WHAT
No Child

MW01484113

There are some very special people in the world, people who truly care about children and teens. This care is seen in so many ways, but today we honor them for their care about and for grieving children and teens.

Parents, teachers, clergy, counselors, pediatricians, coaches, programs, volunteers. The beat goes on. Several have been the pioneers in grief and kids, folks like Earl Grollman, Linda Goldman, The Centering Corporation family, The Abbey Press family, the Dougy Center family, Darcie Sims & Allie Sims Franklin and, with this fine book, Emilio Parga.

Emilio, a man who never seems to tire, is passionate about grieving young people, and this has all come together in their fine program The Solace Tree. Most of all, peer run groups for care and support, with excellent adult support. There also are resources for parents, grandparents and siblings.

Much of this gift, this passion, has come together in the book, *No Child Should Grieve Alone.* New to the field in 2007, this book helps all of us learn more about the grief of kids (and they do grieve!), helps and hugs for parents, and resources for school personnel and community leaders. It is a hands-on, how-to resource all wrapped up in love.

Rev. Richard B. Gilbert, PhD, CT
Director of The World Pastoral Care Center
& Bridge Builders Resources

Emilio's commitment and contribution to grieving children takes yet another leap as he strengthens parents and grief professionals. Accessible and grounded, *No Child Should Grieve Alone* includes an invaluable list of world-wide resources.

Tina Barrett, EdD, LCPC
Co-founder, Center for Integrative Care

Cover design and photo credits: Lisa L. Cook
www.bluemoonpromotions.com

It is only natural that we and our children find many things hard to talk about. But anything human is mentionable and anything mentionable is manageable.

The mentioning can be difficult, and the managing too, but both can be done if we're surrounded by love and trust.

–Fred Rogers, creator and host of Mr. Rogers' Neighborhood

No Child Should Grieve Alone

By Emilio B. Parga, M.A.
Pediatric Thanatologist

Founder/Executive Director
The Solace Tree, Reno, Nevada

www.solacetree.org

ISBN: 1-56123-200-9

The Solace Tree
P.O. Box 2944, Reno, NV 89505

Phone: 775.324.7723, or email us at info@solacetree.org

TABLE OF CONTENTS

Sometimes, I can still see his face and hear his voice, even in my dreams.

Maggie, age 8

ACKNOWLEDGEMENTS

To Mary Bendorfeanu (Bunica) and Bill Parga – THANK YOU.

With the deepest gratitude, Pat Mooney, Donna Schuurman (The Dougy Center) for her love and guidance, Linda Goldman, for her mentorship, Dick Gilbert, whose counsel has been invaluable to The Solace Tree, Joan Schweizer-Hoff for her support, Joan Cochran (The Center for Grief and Loss for Children) for restoring joy in grieving children, Mendy Evans (Judi's House) for always being there, and Janet Sieff and The Centering Corporation team for their unwavering support for this book and its production.

I would like to express my gratitude to the following people for their support to The Solace Tree and the creation of this book: Tammie Anstedt for her boundless passion and commitment in supporting grieving children and adolescents, Wendy Schwedt for her immeasurable time and dedication, Ali Jorgensen for her friendship, Jennifer Benedict and Kathleen Oppio, for believing in grieving children and adolescents, all the volunteers at The Solace Tree, Fuzell-Casey family, Ed Heywood, Janet Higgins and Tim Fanelli, Chris Peto for her time and invaluable assistance in developing our program books, Dr. John Morgan, president of the Graduate Theological Foundation, Heather Woods, Barbara Massey and Gale Hauskins, our principal assistants and research specialists and The FOGs – Riley McHugh, Ben Miller, Larry Barnum, Greg Belancio, Mark Quinlan and Charlie Knight – keep running.

Also, to the many people below who believed in the cause of supporting grieving children and teens: The Washoe County School District, The Washoe County Department of Social Services, Waltons Family of Funeral Homes, Kori McDuffy, Erin Keeton, Kate Langworthy, Joey McNinch, Chris and Eric Breeze of The House of Bread in Reno, NV, Jan Johnson, Renown Health Center, St. Mary's Regional Medical Center, The Alliance of Victims' Rights, Mona and Karen of Sierra Hospice, Jackie Shelton, Lisa Cook of Blue Moon Promotions, Bill Miller, Sally Porterfield, Circle of Life Hospice, Kathy Jacobs, the Solari family, the Allen family, Joseph Galata, Joe Strini, Gary Arlitz, Craig Lemons, Karen Smith the Hunsberger family, the Breen Family, the Clark family, the Cordisco family, the Selby family, Jason Dodd, Bailey Charter and Anderson Elementary School.

To Keeli, a heartfelt thank you and to Hayden who is responsible for the beginning of my life and for lighting up the sky with every breath of my existence.

And most of all, our families at The Solace Tree – Child and Adolescent Center for Grief and Loss, who at the most tender times entrust the care of their children and adolescents to us and who have taught us about the value of peer support groups through their courage, and forward movement in the face of adversity.

Hayden,
you are the light.
Thank you for showing me the way.

To the children,
may you never be alone.

INTRODUCTION

The US Census Bureau estimates that over 2 million children in the United States alone, experience the death of a parent before the age of 18. That means approximately 1 out of every 20 children or teens lose a parent before they graduate from high school. The percentage is much higher when the statistics include other loss experiences that children have, such as death of grandparents, relatives, siblings, caregivers, classmates, teachers, and pets. It is not possible to shield children or protect them from this reality, nor should adults try. Children do grieve and they can be helped with the grieving process. For children, loss is a natural but extremely difficult part of life. Children depend on consistency and stability in their environment in order to reach developmental milestones. Loss and grief can interfere with a child's age appropriate developmental tasks, and may inhibit growth if grief is not allowed safe expression.

In this guidebook you will find helpful information that will deepen your understanding of the emotional components of grief and how to navigate your way through to help children and adolescents. I am convinced that we as teachers become learners. Be encouraged to listen to a child, teen, or adult who is grieving so they know you are present and that you care when they tell you their story of loss. We need to be honest with ourselves and our children. May this book be the start of a conversation on a topic that society often avoids. Most of all, may this book be about education and hope.

PEER SUPPORT GROUPS –
AN APPROACH FOR A PLACE OF HOPE AND HEALING

Peer support groups provide opportunities for expression that helps grieving children and adolescents to understand their day-to-day needs for healing during the grieving process. Peer support groups offer children and teens a safe place to talk about similar feelings, thoughts and experiences, provide emotional, physical, spiritual, and mental support in a nonjudgmental environment and provides a forum to search for meaning about life and death as children and adolescents find normalcy and commonality in their life.

We cannot mistake children's laughter and play after a death for not caring, feeling, or worse, for not having loved the person who died. Children establish their feelings of grief, letting in only what they can handle - a little at a time. Every child and adolescent grieves in their own unique way. As children and teens grieve over time, we must be mindful that they will re-grieve hourly, daily, yearly, maybe forever. As a guide, this book is written from the lessons learned.

Children and adolescents need support from family and friends. Most of all, guidance from caring adults who can help them meet their needs in a supporting environment. Through age appropriate peer support groups children and teens find what is lost, what is left, and what is possible. Through this process, children and adolescents bond and group discussions strengthen, in a safe and secure climate in which information and self-confidence turns adversity into opportunity as they learn about themselves and others. At most, friendships are made, and even in the difficult time of grief, tears and laughter are shared.

Children and teens will eventually need to deal with death. Death, grief and loss are as much a part of life as life itself. Death affects people of all ages. Based on family traditions, values, religion, past losses, support systems and the surviving adult, adults sometimes try to protect children from the natural feelings that accompany the loss of someone or something important. Society can make us feel it is better not to completely be honest about the details of the death and to avoid any important discussion of death. At times we give reasons or make an excuse for our lack of communication, with the belief that children are too young to understand death or can't handle it.

Part One:
Parents and Caregivers

TAKING STOCK ON CHILDREN'S GRIEF

Below are some questions to think about when helping grieving children and adolescents:

- Where are you in your own mortality?
- What language would you use to explain death to children or teens?
- Where is the child (cognitively) in facing the reality of the death?
- What relationship did the child or teen have with the deceased?
- Was the death anticipated or sudden?
- What is your relationship to the deceased?
- What are your spiritual resources?
- Who else has told the child or teen about the death?
- Was the child or teen able to release their emotions?
- What are other support systems for the child or teen?
- Did the child or teen have a chance to say goodbye?
- Was the child allowed to participate in the funeral, memorial or shivah?
- Was there any history of abuse; emotional, physical, or mental?
- Does the child or teen have special needs?
- Is the child or teen on medications?
- Is the child able to grieve and mourn?

There is no formula that tells us how long it will take a child or teen to return to "normal" after a death. No book or doctor can prescribe the way a child or teen should grieve. Regardless, as we take stock of their grief, we have to think about their relationship with the deceased, the age of the child, and the circumstances of the death that play a role in determining the length of times the child or teen will need for his or her healing.

Be present and answer any questions children may have concerning the death. Hold their hand, sit next to them and talk about memories or read a book. Do not be afraid to share or release your own emotions. Let go of any preconceived notions of how children should grieve – Don't lie and do tell what you know of the death, age-appropriately so. Let your child be sad and give them an opportunity to express their emotions through art, play or self-expression. Let them know that in a peer support group they will not be alone and they will learn and grow from other children and teens who are experiencing similar feelings.

The best thing for me was knowing I don't have to talk the nights I go to group. Kids and volunteers just listen. They don't give you advice – they just listen.

– Sharon, 15

HELPING GRIEVING CHILDREN AND TEENS

• At the first opportunity, talk to the parent/caregiver and the children to ask how you can help. Provide parents with regular feedback.

• Acknowledge the child's loss and grief.

• Listen carefully.

• Don't impose your philosophy or theories (stages) of death and grief on a child, no matter how comforting you think it may be. Values, traditions, and religious beliefs surrounding the death are as diverse as children and teens. Give them safety and acceptance, not answers. Remember to be honest, provide routine, give security and show love.

• If appropriate, ask permission to hug the child or teen.

• For children of all ages, plan non-verbal activities to allow expressions of grief. Listen to music, create a dance, draw pictures, act out stories, and collect stones or leaves for opportunities to talk and remember.

• Peer support activities in schools or homes are particularly important for older children. Help students brainstorm what they can do to help their grieving friend.

• Holidays and anniversaries are difficult. Seek ways to acknowledge the deceased.

Kids at school didn't know how to talk to me because they didn't have anybody die. Kids at The Solace Tree understood because they were my age going through the same thing and could relate.
                    –Holly, 12 – An excerpt from a radio interview November 2005

CHILD AND ADOLESCENT DEVELOPMENT

As children and teens grow, they are continually developing skills and awareness that help them assimilate understanding of their losses. **Below is an outline of the child's tasks, concerns, and ways of dealing with death at various developmental stages.**

AGES 0 - 3

Infants and toddlers have no concept of death. They may exhibit more crankiness, clinginess in their behaviors after a death of a parent at this age. It is best to keep daily routines as normal as possible, providing physical assurances; such as, holding, hugging, and being on the floor with them. Grief of young children often goes unrecognized because of their emotional ability to live in the moment. However, children at this age can recognize that something is wrong-or-missing. It is important to monitor their grief in light of their developmental strengths and limits. Some children in this age range may exhibit reactions to loss not necessarily to death but the feeling of emptiness.

AGES 3 - 5

Children grieve through play, art expression, and physical movements. Their imaginations help them wonder about the changes in their lives to struggle with the permanency and causes of death and to notice a parent or caregiver is not around. Children have incomplete verbal abilities and communicate their vulnerability through clinging, unwarranted fears, crying and tantrums. It is imperative we respect our lack of understanding and have trust in a child's ability to heal in his/her own way.

Pictures help me remember.

–Eddie, 5

AGES 6 – 9

Increased verbal skills at this age allow children to articulate their feelings and thoughts more clearly, comprehend the causes and permanency of death, and ask more questions. Their increasing social skills allow them to attain out more significantly to trusted adults and peers, but also create an awareness of their difference from others, and the effect their questions and fears have on others. This is a time to allow children at this age to draw pictures or tell stories about the person who has died.

Nobody understands my loss except the kids who come to group.

–Josh 10

It is most important that children be given honest information about the loss and the changes that are happening in their lives. This is a time when trusted adults outside the family help greatly by answering questions a child or children may have.

Support groups for children at this age who have lost a family member to death are important. Their understanding and comprehension to be alive or to be dead is developing and they are relying on adults to listen to them. Feelings are important and without support for this age group, there may be separation anxiety, destruction, self-destruction and poor school performance. We must give children honest and compassionate answers to reassure that what they are feeling inside is normal. Children do not like to appear different from their peers and joining a peer support group can offer the reassurance that they are not alone.

I feel like I can talk more about my situation since my dad died with others who have gone through what I have gone through.

–A 12 year-old participant

ADOLESCENTS

Being an adolescent is a time of growth and change, often a challenge for everyone even in the best of times. Their cognitive, emotional and physical abilities resemble those of an adult. Adolescents have the ability to comprehend the permanence and vastness of present and past losses. At the same time, they benefit from peer support, hope, knowledge and honest communication.

I can express my feelings and feel comfortable knowing the people in my group won't tell anybody else.

–An 18-year-old participant speaks about the safety during a peer support group in a homicide group after her sister was found dead due to homicide.

THE SPECIAL NEEDS BEREAVED CHILD

In my 15 years working as a volunteer and employee at Marvin Picollo School in Reno, Nevada, and with the Nevada and California Special Olympics, I have found that special needs children have just as many feelings as non-special needs children. They need support, someone who will listen to them, love, understanding, your presence, and caring to affirm their expression of grief. However, depending on their cognitive capacity and relationship with the deceased, they will depend on their ability to grasp the concept of finality and the time to understand the sense of emptiness. We as educators, parents and caregivers must affirm to special needs children that what they are feeling is normal and natural to their loss and it is okay to cry, feel angry and be sad. As we spend a little more time with them, being present, and listening to their story, we can make their grief experience a more worthy one.

Let's not underestimate their presence, emotions, sensitivity, and intelligence. They are very much attuned to the human basic needs. Moreover, they are often quite observant of emotional language and expression. Below are some concerns of grief and mourning patterns of what educators should be aware of when working with special needs children and adolescents following a death in their life:

• Children with special needs form strong attachments to their primary caregiver and other people in their life. Feelings of security, identity, and self-worth are more dependent on the supportive presence of caregivers because of the everyday interaction. When the relationship has been broken because of death, feelings of hopelessness and loss of self are enduring.

• Special needs children can express themselves in an outwardly behavior. You can help them express their grief by giving them outlets – running, bicycling, drawing, hitting pillows, painting, or listening to music. Don't modify behaviors; simply try to recognize the feelings that underline the present behavior of loss and grief.

• Special needs children may feel abandoned, yet have difficulty understanding their loss. We need to give these children a chance to regress, be depressed and act out their grief as well as be with them to answer questions about the death and to provide emotional, mental, and physical outlets.

Special needs children deserve our utmost compassion and support. Please observe, listen and try to understand as they teach us what grief is like for them.

Grief is not a disorder, disease, or sign of weakness. It is an emotional, physical, and spiritual necessity. It is the price you pay for love. The only cure for grief is to grieve.
                                                                    –Earl Grollman

TEACHABLE MOMENTS DURING
AND IMMEDIATELY AFTER A DEATH

Speak to your son or daughter about what has happened as honestly as possible. Use words like dying, death, dead or died. Give them the details you know, tell them what you do not know, and be honest when it is difficult or overwhelming to talk at a certain time.

Consider having a place of honor in your home to set up after the death which is an ever-present reminder of the person's life. Some families light a special candle when they want to honor the deceased, plant a garden, hang a picture of meaning or paint a room or door with special colors. Create a "Memory Book" with your children in which anyone can contribute drawings, pictures, poems or stories. Each of your children might want to have their own, too. Make sure it is a book to which pages can be continually added for a lifetime of memories.

Accept without judgment your child's or teen's feelings about the death, even when the tragedy happens to someone your son or daughter may not have known very well. Young people can be deeply affected by death and crisis in their communities, churches, and sometimes, the world. Often it awakens a sense of vulnerability and the precariousness of life. Allow your son or daughter to talk about the event and express his/her feelings. You can offer the best support by listening to them when they need to share with you how they are feeling.

Sometimes remembering is painful, but not as painful as forgetting.

–Anonymous

Part Two:

*School Personnel, Clergy and Professionals
Working with Bereaved Children
and Adolescents*

SUGGESTIONS FOR SCHOOL PERSONNEL TO HELP GRIEVING STUDENTS AS WELL AS THE FAMILY WHEN DEALING WITH DEATH

When working with bereaved children and adolescents we must be aware of our own beliefs, attitudes, and biases. As we develop an appreciation for cultures and an attitude of comfort, challenge, and satisfaction, we learn that death is universal and that we can continue to grow and learn from bereaved children and teens as they go through life's journey. **Below are suggestions to support grieving children and adolescents:**

• Teachers should find time for open discussion in the classroom to allow students to talk about the death. If you feel uncomfortable attending alone with this, ask your school counselor to step in.

• Your presence at the funeral and/or wake is a priceless comfort to the grieving parents and family. If you feel uncomfortable attending alone, then going with a colleague or group can be helpful. Your presence says a great deal to the family, the community and society.

• Another option for students to express their grief is to write about it. Ask the students to write their memories of the student who died. This can help them process their grief. These notes could be given to the bereaved parents.

• If the child was part of your classroom, have the class create a scrapbook of memories. Then give the memory scrapbook to the bereaved family. Again this can help students deal with their own grief, and it is helpful in reaching out to the family.

• Invite the parents to visit the class and share in the memories. Do not remove the child's desk from the room.

• As educators, try to remember the families during the very difficult times of holidays, birthdays, dates of death through personal notes or other ways of contact. Try to keep the families in mind during the year(s) your student is at school.

Keep in mind that these lists of suggestions are endless and need to be individualized. Acting on any of these ideas, however, is a direct way of teaching respect and an understanding of life. Therefore, as educators, we need to broaden our lessons of learning beyond the textbooks and recognize that grief is part of everyone's life learning process. It is times like these that will demand our flexibility, strength, and understanding as a teacher and friend. Growth and healing can occur if we first recognize the grief and then act upon it in positive and helpful ways. No child should grieve alone.

PREPARING FOR A STUDENTS RETURN
FOLLOWING THE DEATH OF A FAMILY MEMBER

First and foremost, it is helpful to meet with the family in-person prior to their return. Possible meeting times are after school when no students are present or at a home visit. If either are not an option, the telephone is the final option. Utilizing electronic mail is not recommended, as it often makes families feel like "just another number" and is obviously impersonal. It also may lead to a lot of rumors and misunderstandings. First, explain that administrators and support staff are available to support both the parent/caregivers and student(s) in a variety of ways. Explain that school staff will respect the decisions of the entire family regarding what the family chooses to share about the situation. Educate parents on the numerous ways the school can support the family and stress that these are merely suggestions for what the school found to be helpful when addressing the returning students after someone in their life has died. **Below are ways of helping:**

• Ask the parent or caregiver for permission on what you can and cannot say to the children in your classroom about the death.

• Send a letter to the parents or the child's classmates in the classroom of your children about what has happened and have them sign it if they want their child to participate in the discussion about the death of a student or student's parents or caregiver.

• Call in your school counselor or colleagues as a support staff. Discuss what is going to be said.

• Speak with classmates before the student(s) returns.

• Offer an educational 30 minutes at lunch to address the death of a student(s), colleague(s), parent(s) or caregiver(s).

• Have art supplies readily available in the classroom and have children draw or paint when discussing the issue.

• Let them know they can go to the school counselor or their own class to draw, paint or just talk.

• Have literature on hand in the classroom for staff, children, and family members.

• Provide follow-up at the end of the week, month, vacation and school year.

• Debrief as a staff of what happened during the day at school.

GRIEF AND THE CLASSROOM

Maintaining good communication with a child's family in order to remain well informed can also help avoid placing additional stress on a child's coping ability. Quite often a school-age child who has experienced the death of a significant person will exhibit difficult or sympathetic behaviors. These behaviors are normal and may include:

- daydreaming
- disorganization
- trouble completing assignments
- inability to concentrate
- difficulty following directions
- sadness
- procrastination
- restlessness, inability to sit still
- inability to form or maintain friendships

Some of these behaviors can be explained by the simple fact that grieving takes energy. The child may require more sleep than before. Activities that previously came easily, like playing with friends or doing homework, may now become a burden because of limited energy resources.

TEACHABLE MOMENTS
THROUGHOUT THE SCHOOL YEARS

When you see a dead animal or insect, or are establishing an aquarium, discuss the life/death cycle. If a goldfish dies, pause to honor the life in some way by lighting a candle, marking a grave, or talking about living and non-living things.

If you have a pet that is dying or has died, include your children in the process of caring for the pet and sharing information about the illness and death. Allow the children to see the dead body, ask questions, and plan a funeral, even for the smallest pet, such as a fish.

Answer your child's questions about death, loss, and grief in a matter-of-fact way from the earliest age.

Use holidays and life events as opportunities to discuss why people have memorials and why they are important. Most holidays are remembrances of some kind and can open a door for all types of learning and sharing about honoring people after they die.

Honor every goodbye possible in your family: extended absences, separation, divorce, losing a favorite teacher or friend, moving, or the end of the school year. By acknowledging that it is appropriate to grieve all losses, you teach that grief is a natural and healthy response to important change. This is also an opportunity to say goodbye at the end of the school year.

When your child speaks of a loss either aloud, in writing, in play or in his/her artwork, make a time to address the loss. If, for example, your son or daughter shares a memory or a yearning for something or someone who has left or died, stop what you are doing to listen and invite more sharing.

When reading a book which touches on death, pause to talk about it. Many books for children and teens contain events such as deaths, divorces, incarceration, illness and loss of friendships.

As adults, we can come to view loss, both in our families and in the larger community, as "teachable moments." We can help children and teens learn about grieving and the customs people employ to say goodbye to the people and things they love and have lost. In every teachable moment, there is an opportunity to teach our children that; grief is normal, natural and a healthy response to loss. It is important to say goodbye to the people we love.

Part Three:

Living With the Loss

THE DEATH OF A PARENT

No one can fully prepare a child for the death of someone as close as a parent. A child who has lost a parent may be reluctant to leave the other parent to attend school or go to school/sporting events. He or she may worry about the possible death of the surviving parent. A child grieving the death of a parent may experience varying degrees of insecurity, abandonment, guilt, fear and much unresolved pain.

We must remember that the child or teen that loses a parent is probably living with other grieving siblings or adults. Some of the child's emotional needs may go unrecognized. Children can feel obligated to protect the surviving parent or caregiver and may feel responsible for the one who has died. Be aware of the family dynamics.

At times the child may assume the roles of a parent such as meal preparation or helping younger siblings. If the deceased parent had been ill for a while before the death, the child may be confused as he or she experiences relief as well as intense sadness.

THE DEATH OF A SIBLING

Surviving siblings may either constantly talk about the death or they may not want to mention it at all. If a surviving sibling loses a sibling to death in the same school, it may be awhile before they return to school. They may suffer from nightmares, speech disturbances, appetite loss, antisocial tendencies or severe anxiety. Surviving siblings may see resemblances of the deceased in others. Family and friends may idealize the child who has died. This can have a negative effect on surviving siblings' self-esteem and self-reliance.

I sure miss my baby brother; here is a picture of him.
Jimmy, 8 year old participant showing a picture of his brother who died of cancer

THE DEATH OF AN EXTENDED FAMILY MEMBER

Reactions to a death in the extended family (aunt, uncle, cousin, and grandparent) vary greatly depending on the closeness of the relationship. Despite the distance and frequency of visits, it is still a close family member and the child's family will also be grieving. This will, to some degree, affect the child. Regardless of the degree of closeness that child had with the one who died; children need to say goodbye! The child should be given a choice to attend the funeral or memorial. The surviving adult or caregiver should give the child or teen choices in decorating, selecting music, selecting flowers, leaving a note in the casket and what to wear. For some children and teens an extended family member may be the first death in their life. Provide honest answers, security, and listen to what they have to say during this time.

THE DEATH OF SCHOOL FRIENDS
AND SCHOOL PERSONNEL

The impact of the death of a school friend, counselor, teacher or any other staff in the school should not be minimized. Even if the child was not emotionally close to the deceased, that death will cause the child to re-evaluate his or her understanding of death and how it can affect and may trigger past events. A child may wonder, "Who will be next?" A child may feel life is less predictable and not the safe environment he or she once knew. This may be the experience that helps them grasp the finality or eventuality of death, which can be a very scary realization. There will be uncertainty and awkwardness about what to say or what not to say to others. In this manner, children should be able to ask questions and learn they are not alone in their viewpoint.

I know I will never be able to see my dad again, but I know I can be with him in my heart.

–A twelve-year-old participant

THE DEATH OF PETS

Many times the loss of a pet will be the first close experience a child may have with death. This can be very upsetting to the child who cared about their animal. This is an opportunity to teach the child about death, how it can occur, ways the child can say goodbye as well as, remember the pet. Moreover, the grief related to this loss is validated. It also lays a foundation for the child's ability to cope with future losses.

Teach us… that we may feel the importance of every day, of every hour, as is passes.

–Jane Austin, 1811

HOW TO SUPPORT THE GRIEVING CHILD AND TEEN:
A GRIEVING STUDENT

BE CLEAR AND HONEST

Children at almost every age intuitively know when something serious has happened. They observe emotions and expressions; listen in on telephone calls and observe every day routine. Be simple and honest about what happened and use the words "dead" or "died" with an explanation of what death means. Avoid euphemisms such as "Grandpa is sleeping" which can confuse even the oldest child and adult. If you wish to share beliefs about life after death (i.e. "Grandma is in heaven"), do so, after you have shared what you know about death. Let a child's questions lead the way.

RESPECT THEIR NEEDS

When a death is violent, parents and educators automatically hope to protect children and sometimes keep important facts about the loss from them. Yet, we have found that even the youngest child benefits from hearing honest information about the death, even when the death has occurred through suicide or murder. Only when the child or teen is told the truth can he or she begin to understand the death, process the feelings, and integrate the loss into his or her life.

SHARE YOUR GRIEF

It is natural to want to "be strong" for the children, and indeed, it is important not to rely on the child or teen for emotional support. Yet, taking time to talk about loss, share feelings and even cry if you are moved to do so, is truly a gift for children. Sharing grief gives children and teens the courage to share their own feelings and models healthy grieving.

TEACH FEELINGS

Help children identify emotions. Feelings help us know love, sense danger, and mourn our losses. It is part of the nature of feelings to seek expression, which is often how they are healed. Fortunately, feelings also can be stored in our hearts and minds until we can find an appropriate and safe place for expression. By communicating this understanding of feelings, you can validate a child's grief and appreciate grief's expression.

LISTEN. LISTEN. LISTEN.

"Grieving children need compassionate hearts with ears." Be receptive to whatever they say, even if it is very different from what you might expect.

GIVE THEM OPPORTUNITIES FOR EXPRESSION

Find some way to offer outlets for a grieving child that is congruent with your parenting style. Having a place to go when a break is needed, hitting a pillow, journaling to write in feelings, exercise, or creating special projects that relate directly to the deceased are all possibilities. There is no theme; children should be given choices to remember their loved one.

BE UNDERSTANDING – GIVE THEM TIME

As you find the many ways grief manifests itself in children and teens, you can communicate how natural, normal, and healthy this process is. Grieving children need comfort of how they are feeling, thinking, and acting. You can be sympathetic about how difficult it is to concentrate, remember, and focus. Celebrate when even the smallest tasks are accomplished.

REMEMBERING THE LOVED ONE

Simply mention the deceased's name on the anniversary of their death, birth or create a meaningful tradition for those days such as lighting a candle, sharing a meal, or visiting a special spot. It is important to commemorate the person who died. Many people think this will cause pain, but let them know that it's okay when someone actually uses the name in sentences when talking about the person who died. For example, a good friend of mine, Jim Holmes, father of D.J. Benardes who was killed April 2, 1996 in Reno, NV by a man who was drinking and driving, once told me you can never say D.J.'s name enough.

It is natural to yearn for the deceased as the children and adolescents come to milestones such as graduations, weddings, birthdays, holidays and learning to drive, to name a few. It is helpful to invite the family to remember at those times. By remembering and saying the name of the deceased, you honor the love that does not end with death and you validate that grieving continues through life. **Below are a few examples children and adolescents have expressed of what has worked for them when remembering their loved one:**

- Display photographs
- Make a photo album
- Plant a tree
- Sing a song
- Build a bench
- Visit the grave
- Give a donation
- Keep traditions
- Construct new traditions with the deceased in-mind
- Decorate a room
- Make a DVD
- Create a memorial
- Establish a scholarship
- Build a new patio or garden

KEEP IN TOUCH WITH SCHOOL

It can benefit a child or teen greatly to communicate regularly with his/her teacher(s) and counselor. Educators are concerned when they know there has been a death in the family, and appreciate knowing how their student is doing outside of school and how the student can best be helped in the classroom. As the years go by after the death, be sure to inform new teachers and counselors unfamiliar with your family history about your son or daughter's past losses. It will increase their sensitivity and understanding of the child or teen and nurture a partnership of care between you and the school.

Part Four:
Saying Goodbye

FUNERALS, MEMORIALS, SHIVAH AND OTHER CUSTOMS

Many parents struggle over how to best include children and teens in the many rituals and customs employed at the time of death. There are many decisions that are difficult and very personal for each parent and family to make when considering if a child attends a service.

If you were unable to include your children in a way that was agreeable, or you have regrets about how the funeral process unfolded, you can always create a ritual within your family for saying goodbye. Grieving hearts can benefit at any time from a personalized goodbye ceremony. **The following are some ways you can support your child or teen before, during and after the visiting hours, funeral, shivah, memorial service or gathering:**

HONOR THE IMPORTANCE
OF THE RITUALS AND CUSTOMS

At a time of death, young people can be supported by the traditions, religion, customs and rituals that are culturally accepted practice. Although the visiting hours, funeral, or memorial service may be new to them, there can be comfort found in practices that have been done for generations, as well as new traditions created specifically by your family.

As you consider the following suggestions, remember there are many ways to say goodbye as well as know that it is never too late to say goodbye. Children can be easily overlooked. They may have ideas about the songs, poems, pictures or activities the deceased loved and they will undoubtedly always remember which ideas of theirs were contributed. Young people often will want to write a letter or place a drawing in the coffin.

EXPLAIN WHAT TO EXPECT

No matter the age of your child or teen; be sure to explain in specific detail what will happen, and what behavior is expected at the visiting hours, funeral, memorial or service. It is difficult for children to imagine such events, particularly, if they have never attended. It is helpful to explain details such as: what people will wear and why; where a child or teen should stand or sit; what funeral directors and ministers will do; how events will unfold; that other people will be shaking hands, saying "I am sorry" and will look sad.

TALK ABOUT ATTENDING THE FUNERAL OR MEMORIAL

Parents and caregivers may say "no", thinking they are protecting the children when they really are protecting themselves. If possible, try to spend some time sorting out how you feel about your child or teen attending the services before you speak to them about it. Some parents require their sons or daughters to attend; some give their children or teens a choice; others do not feel the child or teen should attend. Children and teens should be included as much as possible in attending the service because it can be meaningful and may help in the healing process. When you talk to children about attending the service, give them reasons for wanting them there or accepting that they may not want to attend. Bring snacks, juice, crayons and a coloring book to keep them occupied in case the funeral or memorial gets lengthy.

TALKING TO CHILDREN ABOUT LEAVING THE FUNERAL OR MEMORIAL

One alternative for families is to ask a child if they want to leave early who would they choose to leave with if the service becomes uncomfortable? This gives the child or teen a sense of control and can alleviate anxiety they may have as they anticipate the event.

DEBRIEFING

It is part of the grieving process to have meaningful memories, regrets, or frustrations about the goodbye rituals. Healing can occur when a young person can express verbally, in writing or through art, what they will remember, what they liked and what they wish could have been different.

FOLLOW UP – A WORD TO THE WISE

Don't forget the children and teens when sending the bereaved family a sympathy card. Let them know that you also are thinking of them during this time of loss.

Provide literature for the family to use that incorporates children's understanding of death, grief and mourning. Check out the national catalog of books for grieving children and families – The Centering Corporation www.centering.org.

Time does not heal a painful loss… Grieving does.

–Anonymous

TAKING CARE OF YOURSELF

There are many ways to care for oneself. Lives are so full; working, raising children, going to school, grieving the death yesterday or grieving the death today. Experiencing any loss is not an easy task. **Below are suggestions from children, teens and adults that have experienced death in their life. Some of the ways to take care of yourself are:**

- Meditating
- Eating healthy
- Staying away from drugs
- Seek healing help – body massage, support groups
- Avoid making major life decisions
- Keeping a journal
- Use destructive ways to vent out your anger
- Writing a letter to the deceased
- Make a memory book
- Make a list of all the things that bring you joy
- Calling someone who will listen
- Exercising
- Resting
- Laughing
- Crying
- Singing
- Dancing

And finding the support you, your child or teen may need is a sign of strength and health to know when you need help. It is not necessary for you to go through this difficult time alone. See our list of resources at the end of this booklet.

Through it all, assure children they are not alone in their feelings of loss.

–Walter Winchell

Part Five:
Resources for Caregivers

**THE NEXT FEW PAGES ARE
GRIEVING CENTERS ACROSS THE GLOBE
COMPILED BY
THE SOLACE TREE in RENO, NV,
AND
THE DOUGY CENTER IN PORTLAND, OR.**

ALABAMA

Amelia Center
1513 4th Ave S
Birmingham, AL 35233
www.ameliacenter.org

Healing House
Community Bereavement Center
425 E Moulton Street SE
Decatur, AL 35601
http://www.hospiceofthevalley.net

Hospice Family Care
3304 Westmill Drive SW
Huntsville, AL 35805
http://www.hospicefamilycare.org

Hospice of Cullman County
402 4th Ave NE
Cullman, AL 35055http://www.
hospiceofcullmancounty.org

Hospice of EAMC
665 Opelika Rd
Auburn, AL 36830
334-826-1899

Hospice of Marshall Co., Inc.
8787 US Highway 431
Albertville, AL 35950
http://www.hospicemc.org

The Caring House
2225 Drake Ave Ste 8
Huntsville, AL 35805
http://www.hospicefamilycare.org

The Healing Place
& Hospice of the Shoals
5604 Ricks Ln
Tuscumbia, AL 35674
http://www.thehealingplaceinfo.org

Wiregrass Hospice Inc.
2740 Headland Ave
Dothan, AL 36303
http://www.wiregrasshospice.org

ALASKA

Forget Me Not Grief Program
500 W International Airport Rd Ste
CAnchorage, AK 99518
http://www.hospiceofanchorage.org

ARIZONA

Children to Children
3922 N Mountain Ave
Tucson, AZ 85719
http://www.tunidito.org

New Song Center
For Grieving Children
6947 East McDonald Dr
Scottsdale, AZ 85253
http://www.thenewsongcenter.org

Parent of Murdered Children, Inc.
P.O. Box 39603
Phoenix, AZ 85069
(602) 254-8818

Safe Harbor Support, Inc.
Gilbert, AZ 85299
(480) 214-5728

Tu Nidito Children & Family Services
3922 N. Mountian
Tucson, AZ 85719
(520) 322-9155

ARKANSAS

Arkansas Children's Hospital
800 Marshall St, Slot 669
Little Rock, AR 72202
http://www.archildrens.org

Center for Good Mourning
800 Marshall Slot 690
Little Rock, AR
(501) 364-7000

Kaleidoscope Kids
1501 North University Ave Ste 680
Little Rock, AR 72207
http://www.kaleidoscopekids.org

CALIFORNIA

After School Counseling Services
1515 Floribunda Ave Ste 305
Burlingame, CA 94010

Camarillo Hospice
400 Rosewood Avenue
Camarillo, CA 92677
(805) 389-6870

**Camp Good Grief -
Loma/Linda University**
11234 Anderson Street, Rm 1901
Loma Linda, CA 92354
(909) 558-4073

CASA of Siskenyon County
P.O. Box 1337
Yreka, CA 96097
(530) 841-0369

Centre for Living with Dying
1265 El Camino Real Ste 208
Santa Clara, CA 95050
http://www.thecentre.org

Children's Bereavement Art Group
2800 L St Ste 400
Sacramento, CA 95816
916-454-6555

Circle of Care
2540 Charleston St
Oakland, CA 94602
http://www.ebac.org

Comfort for Kids
2051 Harrison ST
Concord, CA 94520
http://www.hospicecc.org

Common Threads At Inland Hopsice
233 W. Harrison
Claremont, CA 91711
(909) 399-3289

Community Hospice, Inc.
601 McHenry Ave
Modesto, CA 95350
http://www.hospiceheart.org

Contra Costa Crisis Center
PO Box 3364
Walnut Creek, CA 94598
http://www.crisis-center.org

Drew's Place
138 New Mohawk # 6
Nevada City, CA 95959
http://www.drewsplace.net

Elizabeth Hospice
150 W Crest St
Escondido, CA 92025
http://www.elizabethhospice.org

Footsteps at Saint Agnes Medical Center
1303 E Herndon
Fresno, CA 93720
http://www.samc.com

Gary's Place for Kids
23332 Mill Creek Dr, Ste 230
Laguna Hills, CA 92653
http://www.garysplaceforkids.org

Good Grief for Kids
23625 Holman Hwy
Monterey, CA 93942
http://www.chomp.org

Grief Recovery Institute
PO Box 6061-382
Sherman Oaks, CA 91413
http://www.grief-recovery.com

**Griefbusters
Hospice of the Central Coast**
945 S Main St Ste 101
Salinas, CA 93901
http://www.chomp.org

Griefbusters of Amador
PO Box 595
Jackson, CA 95642
209-223-5500

Heartland Home, Health Care & Hospice
1700 Iowa Avenue
Riverside, CA 92507
(951) 369-8640

Hinds Hospice Center for Grief and Loss
1616 W. Shaw, Ste. B-6
Fresno, CA 93711
(559) 248-8579

Hope Bereavement Center
5441 Avenida Encinas, Suite A
Carlsbad, CA 92008
(760) 431-4100

Hospice of the Conejo
80 E. Hillcrest #204
Thousand Oaks, CA 91360
(805) 495-2145

Hope Hospice
6500 Dublin Blvd, Ste 100
Dublin, CA 94568
http://www.HopeHospice.com

Hospice of Hunboldt Bereavement Services
2010 Myrtle Avenue
Eureka, CA 95501
(707) 445-8445

Hospice of Marin
Youth Bereavement Program
150 Nellen Ave
Corte Madera, CA 94925
http://www.hospiceofmarin.org

Hospice of Napa Valley, Inc.
404 S. Jefferson St.
Napa, CA 94559
(707) 258-9080

Hospice of Petaluma
Children and Teen Program
416 Payran St.
Petaluma, CA 94952
707-778-6242

Hospice of San Luis Opisbo Country, Inc.
1304 Pacific St
San Luis Opisbo, CA 93401
http://www.hospiceslo.org

Hospice of the North Coast
Community Outreach
5441 Avenida Encinas, Ste A
Carlsbad, CA 92008
http://www.hospicenorthcoast.org

Hospice of the Valley
1150 S. Bascom Avenue, Ste. 7A
San Jose, CA 95128
(408) 947-1233

Hospice of Ukiah - Children's Program
P.O. Box 914
Ukiah, CA 95482
(707) 462-4038

H.U.G. (Health Understanding
of Grief) of Hospice
940 Disc Drive
Scotts Valley, CA 95066
(831) 430-3000

Inland Hospice Association
233 W. Harrison Avenue
Claremont, CA 91711
(909) 399-3289

International Network
for Attitudinal Healing
33 Buchanan Dr.
Sausalito, CA 94965
http://www.attitudinalhealing.org

Josie's Place
265 Lexington Street
San Francisco, CA 94110
(415) 695-0642

KARA Grief Support
457 Kingsley Ave
Palo Alto, CA 94301
http://www.kara-grief.org

Kaiser Hospice
2025 Morse Avenue
Sacramento, CA 95825
(916) 486-5300

Kaiser - Permanente Hospice
12200 Bellflower Blvd.
Downey, CA 90242
(562) 622-4317

New Hope Grief Support Community
P.O. Box 8057
Long Beach, CA 90808
(562) 429-0075

Odyssey Healthcare, Inc.
71777 San Jacinto Drive, Ste. 201
Palm Desert, CA 92270
(760) 346-2816

Our House-A Grief Support Center
1950 Sawtelle Blvd Ste 255
Los Angeles, CA 90025
http://www.ourhouse-grief.org

Our House-A Grief Support Center
22801 Ventura Blvd Ste 112
Woodland Hills, CA 91364
http://www.ourhouse-grief.org

Pathways Volunteer Hospice
3300 E South St Ste 206
Long Beach, CA 90805
http://www.aboutpathways.com

Sharp Hospice Care
4000 Ruffin Rd, Ste A
San Diego, CA 92123
http://www.sharp.com

San Diego Hospice & Palliative Care
4311 Thrid Avenue
San Diego, CA 92103
(619) 688-1600

Sutter VNA and Hospice
Children's Services
1110 N Dutton Ave
Santa Rosa, CA 95401
http://www.suttervnaandhospice.org

The Center for Grief and Loss
924 West 70th St
Los Angeles, CA 90044
http://www.griefcenterforchildren.org

The Center for Grief and Loss
37 N Holliston
Pasadena, CA 91106
http://www.griefcenterforchildren.org

The Center for Grief and Loss
1010 N Central
Glendale, CA 91202
http://www.griefcenterforchildren.org

The Gathering Place
514 N Prospect #115
Redondo Beach, CA 90277
http://www.griefcenter.net

The Healing Center for Grieving Children
7680 Shelborne Drive
Granite Bay, CA 95746
(916) 791-8414

The Healing Center for Grieving Children
7560 Florin Rd
Sacramento, CA 95828
http://www.grievingchild.net

The Mourning Star Center
of the VNAIC
42600 Cook St Ste 202
Palm Desert, CA 92260
http://www.mourningstar.org

Touchstone Support Network
3041 Olcott St
Santa Clara, CA 95054
http://www.php.com

Willmar Center for Bereaved Children
PO Box 1374
Sonoma, CA 95476

http://www.willmarcenter.org
Wings of Hope
1717 S Main St
Lakeport, CA 95453
http://www.hospice-lakecountyca.org

Yolo Hospice
PO Box 1014
Davis, CA 95617
http://www.yolohospice.org

COLORADO

Camp Comfort
P.O. Box 2880
Evergreen, CO 80437
(303) 674-6400

Center for Loss and Life Transition
3735 Broken Bow Rd
Fort Collins, CO 80526
http://www.centerforloss.com

Healing Circle
A Program of Hospice Care of Boulder
2594 Trailing Dr East, Ste. A
Lafayette, CO 80026
(303) 604-5330

Healing Circles
1235 Pine St
Boulder, CO 80302
http://www.hospicecareonline.org

Hospice and Palliative Care
of Western Colorado
2754 Compass Dr, Ste 377
Grand Junction, CO 81506
http://www.gvhospice.com

Hospice of Metro Denver
501 S. Cherry St. Ste. 700
Denver, CO 80246
http://www.hmd.org

House for Grieving Children
PO Box 621632
Littleton, CO 80162

Judith Ann Griese Foudation
1600 Downing St., Ste. 200
Denver, CO 80218
(720) 941-0331

Judi's House
1741 Gaylord St
Denver, CO 80206
http://www.judishouse.org

Mt. Evans Hospice
PO Box 2770
Evergreen, CO 80437
http://www.campcomfort.org

Pathways Bereavement Services
1716 Reading
Pueblo, CO 81001
(719) 296-6205

**Sangre De Crisco Hospice
& Palliative Care**
1207 Pueblo Blvd Wy
Pueblo, CO 81005
http://www.pueblohospice.org

CONNECTICUT

Reginal Hospice of Western CT
405 Main St
Danbury, CT 06810
http://www.danbury.org/hospice/children

**Healing Hearts Center for
Grieving Children and Famlies**
405 Main Street
Danbury, CT 06810
(203) 792-4422

Mary's Place
6 Poquonock Ave
Windsor, CT 06095
http://www.marysplacect.com

The Center for Hope, Inc
590 Post Rd
Darien, CT
http://www.centerforhope.org

The Cove Center for Grieving Children
134 State St
Meriden, CT 06450
http://www.covect.org

The Cove/West Hartford
854 Farmington Ave
West Hartford, CT 06119
860-233-1700

The Den for Grieving Kids
40 Arch St
Greenwich, CT
http://www.family centers.org\children

DELAWARE

Delaware Hospice
600 DuPont Hwy Ste 107
Georgetown, DE 19947
http://www.delawarehospice.org

**Supporting Kidds
The Center for Grieving Children**
1213 Old Lancaster Pike
Hockessin, DE 19707
(302) 235-5544

Supporting K.I.D.D.S.
PO Box 7543
Wilmington, DE 19803
http://www.supportingkidds.org

D.C.

Wendt Center for Loss and Healing
730 Eleventh St NW 3rd Floor
Washington, DC 20001
http://www.wendtcenter.org

FLORIDA

Begin Again Children's Grief Center
1124 Beville Rd Ste C
Baytona Beach, FL 32114
386-258-5100

**Bethany Center
of Good Sheperd Hospice**
50 Lake Morton Dr
Lakeland, FL
http://www.thebethanycenter.org

**Bright Star Center
for Grieving Children**
300 E. New Haven Avenue
Melborne, FL 32901
(321) 733-7672

**Caring Tree Program
of Big Bend Hospice**
1723 Mahan Center Blvd
Tallahassee, FL 32308
http://www.bigbendhospice.org

Catholic Hospice
14160 Palmetto Frontage Rd Ste 100
Miami Lakes, FL 33016
http://www.catholichospice.org

Children's Bereavement Center
7600 South Red Rd Ste 307
South Miami, FL 33143
http://www.childbereavement.org

**Circle of Love
Center for Grieving Children**
3010 W Azeele St
Tampa,FL 33609
http://www.lifepath-hospice.org

**Community Hospice
of Northeast Florida**
4266 Sumbeam Rd
Jacksonville, FL 03257
http://www.communityhospice.com

Gulfside Regoinal Hospice
6224 Lafayetter Street
N.P.R., FL 34652
(727) 844-3946

Hearts and Hope, Inc.
317 10th St
West Palm Beach, FL 33401
http://www.heartsandhope.org

Hope Hospice Rainbow Center
9470 HealthPark Circle
Fort Myers, FL 33908
http://www.hopehospice.org

Horizons Berevement Center
5300 East Ave
West Palm Beach, FL 33407
http://www.hpbc.com

Horizons Children's Loss Program
595 Montgomery Road
Altamonte Spring, FL 32714
(407) 682-5737

Hospice by the Sea, Inc.
1531 W Palmetto Park Rd
Boca Raton, FL 33486
http://www.hospicebytheseafl.org

Hospice of Citrus County
PO Box 641270
Beverly Hills, FL 34464

http://www.hospiceofcitruscounty.org
Hospice of Lake Sumter, Inc.
12300 Lane Park Rd
Tavares, FL 32778
http://www.hospicels.com

Hospice of ST. Francis
2395 South Washington Ave
Titusville, FL 32780
http://www.hospiceofstfrancis.com

Hospice of the Emerald Coast
2925 MLK Blvd
Panama City, FL 32405
http://www.hospiceemeraldcoast.org

**Kathy's Place
A Center for Grieving Children**
730 S. Sterling Ave., #301
Tampa, FL 33609
(813) 875-0728

Lee's Place, Inc.
216 Lake Ella Dr
Tallahassee, FL 32303
http://www.leesplace.org

New Hope for Kids
900 North Maitland Ave
Maitland, FL 32751
http://www.newhopeforkids.org

North Star
1250-B Grumman Place
Titusville, FL 32780
(321) 264-1687

**The Bright Star
Center for Grieving Children**
300 E New Haven Ave
Melbourne, FL 32901
321-733-7672

**The Bethany Center
of Good Shepherd Hospice**
50 Lake Morton Drive
Lakeland, FL 33801
(863) 802-0456

The Children's Bereavement Center
Miami, FL 33143

VNA/ Hospice
1110 35th Lane
Vero Beach, FL 32960
(772) 978-5558

HAWAII

Hospice Hawaii
860 Iwlilei Rd
Honolulu, HI 96817
http://www.hospicehawaii.org

Kauai Hospice
PO Box 3286
Lihue, HI 96766
http://www.kauaihospice.org

Kids Hurt Too
PO Box 11260
Honolulu, HI 96828
http://www.grievingyouth.org

Hospice of Hilo
1011 Waianuenue Avenue
Hilo, HI 96720
http://www.hospiceofhilo.org

Outreach for Grieving Youth Alliance
P.O. Box 11260
Honolulu, HI 96828
(808) 735-2989

IDAHO

Bonner Community Hospice
PO Box 1448
Sandpoint, ID 83864
http://www.bonnergen.org

Gritman Medical Center
700 South Main St
Moscow, ID 83843
http://www.gritman.org

Kids Count Too
826 Eastland Dr
Twin Falls, ID 83301
208-734-4061

Touchstone
The Center for Grieving Children
1500 W Hays
Boise, ID 83702
http://www.touchstonecenter.org

Willow Center
PO Box 1361
Lewiston, ID 83501
http://www.willow-center.org

ILLINOIS

Buddy's Place
1023 W Burlington Ave
Western Springs, IL 60558
http://www.ccoptions.org

Center for Grief Recovery
1263 W Loyola, Ste 100
Chicago, IL 60626
http://www.griefcounselor.bigstep.com

Fox Valley Hospice
& Care for the Bereaved
200 Whitfield Dr.
Geneva, IL 60134
http://www.foxvalleyhospice.net

Heartlight
2300 Children's Plaza
Chicago, IL 60614
http://www.childrensmemorial.org

Institute for Juvenile Research
907 S Wolcott
Chicago, IL 60612
312-413-0997

Kid's Time Grief Support Group
211 S Third St
Belleville, IL 62222
http://www.steliz.org

Kids Clubhouse
Five 157 Center
Edwardsville, IL 62025
618-656-1600

Palliative Carecenter
& Hospice of the North Shore
2821 Central St
Evanston, IL 60201
847-467-7423

Rainbows, Inc. International
2100 Golf Road, Unit 370
Rolling Meadows, IL 60008
http://www.rainbows.org

The Heart Connection
2800 W 95th St
Evergreen Park, IL 60805
http://www.lcmh.org

The Ramona Connection
233 W Cumberland
Martinsville, IL 62442
217-382-6684

Willow House
80 Oakwood Lane
Lincolnshire, IL 60069
http://www.willowhouse.org
http://www.ryans-place.org

INDIANA

Brooke's Place
for Grieving Young People, Inc.
50 E 91st St., Ste. 103
Indianapolis, IN 46240
http://www.brookesplace.org

Center for Hospice & Palliative Care
215 Red Coach Drive
Mishawaka, IN 46545
(574) 255-1064

Erin's House for Grieving Children, Inc.
3811 Illinois Rd Ste 210
Fort Wayne, IN 46804
http://www.erinshouse.org

Gateway Hospice/Camp Willow Creed
1760 Madison Street
Clarksville, IN 37043
(931) 648-4576

Healing Hearts Grief Suppost Group
600 Superior Ave.
Munster, IN 46321
(219) 922-2732

Health Ministry Partnership
1328 Draygon Tri
Mishawaka, IN 46544
(574) 254-0454

Henry County Memorial Hospital
Hospice
798 N. 16th Street
New Castle, IN 47362
(765) 593-2389

Hippensteel Funeral Home
822 N. 9th Street
Lafayette, IN 47904
(765) 742-7302

Hospice of Dearborn Co. Hospital
370 Bielby Road
Lawrenceburg, IN 47025
(812) 537-8192

Hospice of the Wabash Valley
600 S. 1st Street
Terre Haute, IN 47807
(812) 234-2515

Jasper County Hospital HHC & Hospice
1104 E. Grace
Rensselaer, IN 47987
(219) 866-5141

Kosciunko Home Care & Hospice
902 Provident Drive
Warsaw, IN 46580
(574) 372-3401

Legacy House, Inc.
2505 N. Arlington Ave.
Indianapolis, IN 46218
(317) 554-5272

Living with Grief Support Group
P.O. Box 279
Winamac, IN 46996
(574) 946-2100

Pulaski Memorial Hospital
Dept. of Oncology
616 E 13th Street, P.O. Box 279
Winamac, IN 46996
(574) 983-3344

Mending Hearts
1407 S 8th St
Richmond, IN 47374
http://www.bgcrichmond.org

Reid Hospital
& Health Care Services Hospice
1401 Chester Blvd.
Richmond, IN 47374
(765) 983-3344

Ryan's Place
PO Box 73
Goshen, IN 46527
http://www.ryans-place.org

Serenity Hospice
103 S. Grant Avenue
Fowler, IN 47944

(765) 884-7000
State of the Heart Hospice
410 W. Votaw Street
Portland, IN 47371
(260) 726-3220

The Center for Mental Health
Anderson, IN 46012
(765) 649-8061

Visiting Nurse & Hospice Home
5910 Homestead Road
Fort Wayne, IN 46814
(260) 435-3222

Vista Care Hospice
391 Quatermaster Court
Jeffersonville, IN 47130
(812) 284-2600

Iowa

Amanda The Panda
1000 73rd St Ste 12
Des Moines, IA 50311
http://www.amandathepanda.org

Children's Grief Support
505 Union
Pella, IA 50219
(641) 620-5050

Grief Support Services
P.O. Box 2880
Waterloo, IA 50704
(517) 272-2002

Iowa City Hospice
1025 Wade Street
Iowa City, IA 52240
(319) 351-5665

Eucalyptus Tree Program
PO Box 2880
Waterloo, IA 50704
http://www.cvhospice.org

Rick's House of Hope for Grieving
1227 East Rusholme St
Davenport, IA 52803
http://www.genesishealth.com

Kansas

Solace House
8012 State Line Rd Ste 202
Shawnee Mission, KS 66208
http://www.solacehouse.org

Three Trees Center
8100 East 22nd St N
Building 800, Ste 100
Wichita, KS 67226
http://wwwthreetrees.org

Kentucky

Bridges Center
2120 Newburg Rd, Ste 200
Louisville, KY 40205
http://www.hospices.org

Community Hospice
1538 Central Avenue
Ashland, KY 41101
(606) 329-1890

Drawbridges
313 W Madison St
La Grange, KY 40031
http://www.drawbridges.com

**Hospice & Palliative Care
of Central Kentucky**
105 Diecks Dr
PO 2149
Elizabethtown, KY 42702
270-737-6300

Hospice of the Bluegrass
2312 Alexandria Dr
Lexington, KY 40504
http://www.hospicebg.com

RENEW: Center for Personal Recovery
PO Box 125
136 Ridge Ave
Berea, KY 40403
http://www.renew.net

St. Anthony's Hospice
2410 S. Green Street
Henerson, KY 42420
(270) 826-2326

St. Claire Hospice
222 Medical Circle
Morehead, KY 40351
(606) 783-6808

Stars Program
2718 Dixie Hwy
Crestview Hills, KY 41017
http://www.starsforchildren.com

LOUISIANA

A Place That Warms the Heart
3410 Shadow Wood Dr
Haughton, LA 71037

Project Sky/Grief Recovery Center
4919 Jamestown Ave Ste 102
Baton Rouge, LA 70808
225-924-6621

Seasons Grief Center
654 Brockenbraugh Court
Metairie, LA 70005
http://www.seasonsgriefcenter.org

The Healing House
PO Box 3861
Lafayette, LA 70502
http://www.healing-house.org

MAINE

Grieving Children's Program
150 Dresden Ave
Gardiner, ME 04345
http://www.hospicevolunteerskennebec.org

A Program for Greiving Children & Teens
P.O. Box 819
Lewiston, ME 04243
(207) 777-7740

Healing Circle for Grieving Children
P.O. box 688
Caribou, ME 04736
(207) 498-2578

Hospice Volunteers
45 Baribeau Dr
Brunswick, ME 04011
http://www.hospicevolunteers.org

Hospice Volunteers of Waterville
Area304 Main St
Waterville, ME 04901
http://www.hvwa.org

Pathfinders: Hospice of Eastern Maine
885 Union St Ste 220
Bangor, ME 04401
http://www.emh.org

Program for Grieving Children & Teens
15 Strawberry Ave
Lewiston, ME 04243
207-777-7740

The Center for Grieving Children
49 York St
Portland, ME 04101
http://www.cgcmaine.org

MARYLAND

**Bridges/Calvert Hospice Care
and Resource Center**
238 Merrimac Ct
Prince Frederick, MD 20678
http://www.calverthospice.org

Carroll Hospice
95 Carroll St
Westminster, MD 21157
http://www.carrollhospitalcenter.org

Hospice of Charles County, Inc.
105 La Grange Ave
Po Box 1703
http://www.hospiceofcharlescounty.org

Hospice of Frederick County
PO Box 1799
Frederick, MD 21702
http://www.hospiceoffrederickco.com

Hospice of the Chesapeake
445 Defense Highway
Annapolis, MD 21401
http://www.hospicechesapeake.org

Me Too/ Stella Maris, Inc.
2300 Dulaney Valley Rd
Timonium. MD 21093
http://www.stellamarisinc.com

Montgomery Hospice
1355 Piccard Dr Ste 100
Rockville, MD 20850
http://www.montgomeryhospice.org

Teens Learning to Grieve
2914 East Joppa Rd, Ste 204
Baltimore, MD 21234
410-665-5550

MICHIGAN

Ashley's Friends
1875 Eager Road
Howell, MI
(517) 546-4440

Barry Community Hospice
450 Meadow Run, Ste. 200
Hastings, MI 49058
(269) 948-8452

Braveheart Grief Center
126 Main Centre
Northville, MI 48167
http://www.braveheartofmichigan.org

Ele's Place
1145 W Oakland Ave
Lansing, MI 48915
http://www.elesplace.org

Gilda's Club Grand Rapids
1806 Brodge Street NW
Grand Rapids, MI 49504
(616) 453-8300

Gilda's Club Mento Detroit
3517 Rochester Road
Royal Oak, MI 48334
(248) 577-0800

Gratiot Area Hospice
300 Warwick Drive
Alma, MI 48801
(989) 466-3214

Healing Hearts
Hospice of Helping Hands, Inc.
335 E. Houghton Ave.
West Branch, MI 48661
(989) 345-4700

Heartland Hospice
1426 Strais Drive
Bay City, MI 48706
(800) 275-4517

Hospice at Home Inc.
4025 Health Park Lane
Saint Joseph, MI 49085
http://www.hospiceathome.org

Hospice of Lenawee
415 Mill Rd
Adrian, MI 49221
517-263-2323

Hospice Care of SW Michigan
Journeys of Grief
222 N. Kalamazoo Mall Ste. 100
Kalamazoo, MI 49007
(269) 345-0273

Hospice of Hillsdale County
124 South Howell Street
Hillsdale, MI 48734
(517) 437-5252

Hospice of Hope
Lutheran Home Care Agency
9710 Junction Road
Frankenmuth, MI 48734
(989) 652-4663

Hospice of Little Traverse Bay
Children's Bereavement
34343 M-119, Suite F
Harbor Springs, MI 49740
(231) 487-7233

Hospice of Michigan
2525 Telegraph Road
Bloomfield Hill, MI 48302
(248)253-2580

Hospice of Michigan
Grief Support Services
1260 Erhart NE
Grand Rapids, MI 49503
(616) 356-5253

Lifespan Good Samaritan Hospice
166 E. Goodale Avenue
Battle Creek, MI 49017
(269) 660-3621

Lory's Place
445 Upton Drive
St. Joseph, MI 49085
(269) 983-2707

Memorial Healthcare Hospice
1488 N M-52
Owosso, MI 48867
(989) 725-2299

Mid Michigan Visiting Nurse
Association Hospice
3007 N. Saginaw Road
Midland, MI 48640
(989) 633-1400

Project HUGG:
Helping Us Grow and Grieve
520506 Hunt Club Drive
Harper Woods, MI 48225

Mercy Memorial Hospice of Monroe
725 Monroe St
Monroe, MI 48162
http://www.mercymemorial.org

Mourning Kids
William Beaumont Hospital
44201 Dequindre
Troy, MI 48098
http://www.beaumonthospital.com

New Hope Center for Grief Support
113 E Dunlap
Northville, MI 48167
http://www.newhopecenter.net

Open Arms
A Grieving Children's Program
11148 Harper Ave
Detroit, MI 48213
http://www.stjohn.org/openarms

Pathfinders: Grief Support for Children
331 N Center
Northville, MI 48167
http://www.arborhospice.org

Pathfinders: Grief Support for Children
2366 Oak Valley Dr
Ann Arbor, MI 48103
http://www.arborhospice.org

Pathfinders: Support Services for Children
19145 Allen Rd #110
Trenton, MI 48183
http://www.arborhospice.org

SandCastles Grief Support Program
1 Ford PI Ste 2a
Detroit, MI 48202
http://www.aboutsandcastles.org

Saint Joseph Mercy Livingston Hospice
907 Fowler Street
Howell, MI 48843
(517) 540-9125

The Loft at Hospice of Holland, Inc.
270 Hoover Blvd.
Holland, MI 49423
(616) 396-2972

Three Rivers Health Hospice
633 S. Erie St.
Three Rivers, MI 49093
(269) 278-6108

Visiting Nurse Services of Michigan
825 E. Michigan Avenue
Lansing, MI 48912
(517) 367-5922

Visiting Nurse Services
of Michigan Bay
Essexville, MI 48732
(989) 895-4701

Vital Care Hospice of the Sunrise Shore
1691 M-32 West, Ste 100
Alpena, MI 49707
(989) 358-1156

MINNESOTA

Children's Hospitals and Clinics
345 N Smith Ave
Saint Paul, MN 55102
612-813-6622

Minnesota Valley Youth Grief Services
201 E Nicollette Blvd
Burnsville, MN 55337
952-892-2111

Minnesota Youth Grief Coalition
201 E Nicollette Blvd
Burnsville, MN 55337

952-892-2112
St. Mary's Grief Support Center
407 E 3rd St
Duluth, MN 55805
218-786-4402

The Healing Quilt
2525 Chicago Ave S
Minneapolis, MN 55404
http://www.childrenshc.org

MISSISSIPPI

McClean Fletcher Center
2624 Southerland St
Jackson, MS
http://www.jljackson.org

MISSOURI

Annie's Hope
The Bereavement Center for Kids
1333 W. Lockwood, Suite 104
St. Louis, MO 63122
(314) 965-5051

KAPstone House Inc.
2004 S Joplin
Joplin, MO
417-206-4700

Lost and Found:
A Place for Hope and Grief
1201 E Walnut St
Springfield, MO 65802
http://www.lostandfoundozarks.com

St. Louis Bereavement
Center for Young
422 S Clay
Kirkland, MO 63122

The Missouri Baptist Medical Center
3015 N Ballas Rd
Saint Louis, MO 63131
http://www.missouribaptistmedicalcenter.org

MONTANA

Peace Hospice of Montana
Children's Bereavement
1101 26th Ave. South
Great Falls, MT 59405
(406) 455-3040

NEBRASKA

Charlie Brown's Kids-Good Grief
PO Box 67106
Lincoln, NE 68506
402-483-1845

Mourning Hope Grief Center
7142 S 45th St
Lincoln, NE 68516
http://www.mourninghope.org

Ted E. Bear Hollow
PO Box 4823
Omaha, NE 68104
402-502-2773

NEVADA

The Solace Tree
Child and Adolescent Center
for Grief and Loss
PO Box 2944, Reno, Nevada 89505
(775) 324-7723
www.solacetree.org

Horizon Hospice
P.O. Box 5361
Elko, Nevada 89802

Nathan Adelson Hospice
4141 Swenson St
Las Vegas, NV 89119
www.nah.org

NEW HAMPSHIRE

Bridges for Children & Teens
10 Hampton Rd
Exeter, NH 03833
http://www.seacoasthospice.org

Good Mourning Children
54 Blackberry Ln
Keene, NH 03431
603-352-7799

Hospice Bereavement Program at HCS
312 Marlborough Street
Keene, NH 03431
(603) 352-2253

Hospice at HCS
69 Island St
Keene, NH 03431
http://www.hcsservices.org

Hospice of Cheshire County
7 Center St
Keene, NH 03431
603-257-1314

Pete's Place
1 Webb Pl Ste 6
Dover, NH 03820
603-740-2689

Victims, Inc.
P.O. Box 455
Rochester, NH 03866
(603) 335-7777

**VNA of Manchester
and Southern New Hampshire**
1850 Elm St
Manchester, NH 03104
http://www.manchestervna.org

New Jersey

**Children's Art Therapy Program
at Riverview**
1 Riverview Plaza
Red Bank, NJ 07701
(732) 530-2382

Comfort Zone Camp North
46 Brookside Terrace
North Caldwell, NJ 01006
(201) 420-0081

Good Grief, Inc.
P.O. Box 763
Summit, NJ 07901
(908) 251-5101

Griefwork Center, Inc.
PO Box 5104
Kendall Park, NJ 08824
http://www.griefworkcenter.com

JFK Medical Center
65 James St
Edison, NJ 08818
http://www.jfkmc.com

**Sudden Unexplained
Death in Childhood Program**
30 Porspect Ave
Hackensack, NJ 07601
973-783-2590

The Alcove Center for Grieving Children & Families
950 Tilton Rd
Northfield, NJ 08225
http://www.thealcove.org

The Children's Art Therapy Program
1 Riverview Plaza
Red Bank, NJ 07701
http://www.meridianhealth.com

**Wings of Hope Programs for
Continuing Support Services**
P.O. Box 443
Medford, NJ 08055
(609) 714-0868

New Mexico

Children's Grief Center of New Mexico, Inc.
PO Box 20218
Albuquerque, NM 87154
http://childrensgrief.org

Gerard's House
PO Box 28693
Santa Fe, NM 87592
http://www.gerardshouse.org

Golden Willow Retreat
P.O. Box 569
Arroyo Hondo, NM 87513
(505) 776-2024

NM Survivors of Homicide, Inc.
12400 Menaul Blvd. NE, Ste 100
Albuquerque, NM 87112
(505) 232-4099

**The Greater Albuquerque
Compassionate Friends**
12400 Menaul Blvd. NE, Ste 100
Albuquerque, NM 87112
(505) 232-4099

New York

**American Foundation
for Suicide Prevention**
120 Wall St 22nd Floor
New York, NY 10005
212-363-3500

Calvary Hospital
1740 Eastchester Rd
Bronx, NY 10461
http://www.calvaryhospital.org

**Catskill Area Hospice
and Palliative Care, Inc.**
542 Main St
Oneonta, NY 13820
http://www.cahpc.org

Center for Hope
270-06 76th Ave
New Hyde Park, NY 11040
718-470-3123

Center for Living with Loss
990 Seventh North St
Liverpool, NY 13088
http://www.hospicecny.org

Circle of Daughters, Inc.
4637 Ironwood Dr
Hamburg, NY 14075
http://www.circleofdaughters.com

Good Sheperd Hospice
4747-20 Nesconset Hwy
Port Jefferson Station, NY 11776
631-474-4040

Haven Grief Counseling Center
703 Union St
Schenectady, NY 12305
http://www.havengriefcounselingcenter.org

Heartbridge
711 West End Ave Ste 6ls
New York, NY 10025
http://www.heartbridgecenter.org

Hope for the Bereaved, Inc.
4500 Onondaga Blvd
Syracuse, NY 13219
http://www.hopeforbereaved.com

Hospice Care Network
900 Merchants Concourse
Westbury, NY 11590
http://www.hospicecarenetwork.org

**Jewish Board of Family
& Children Services**
120 W 57th St, 9th Fl

New York, NY 10019
http://www.jbfcs.org
Kids Cape Camp
108 Steelue Avenue
Glovesville, NY 12078
(518) 725-4545

Metropolitan Hospice of Greater New York
6323 Seventh Ave
Brooklyn, NY 11220
http://www.metropolitanhospice.org

New Insights, Inc.
PO Box 5027
Saratoga Springs,NY 12866
518-893-2012

South Nassau Communities Hospital
2277 Grand Ave
Baldwin,NY 11510
516-546-1370

St. Mary's Hospital for Children
29-01 216th St
Bayside, NY 11360
http://www.stmaryskids.org

Storm Clouds & Rainbows
3580 Harlem Rd
Buffalo, NY 14215
http://www.palliativecare.org

The Bereavement Center
374 Violet Ave
Poughkeepsie, NY 12601
http://www.hospiceinc.org

The Bereavement & Trauma Center
480 Old Westbury Rd.
Roslyn Heights, NY 11577
(516) 299-5373

The Bereavment Center of Westchester
69 Main Street
Tuckahoe, NY 10708
(914) 961-2818

The Caring Circle
45 Park Ave
Yonkers, NY 10701
http://www.hospiceofwestchester.com

The Caring Circle
100 S Bedford Rd Fl 3
Mount Kisco, NY 10549
http://www.hospiceofwestchester.com

The Children's Grieving Center
800 Stony Brook Ct
Newburgh, NY 112550
http://www.hospiceoforange.com

The Healing Center
339 Hicks St
Brooklyn, NY 11201
http://www.healingcenterkids.org

The Health Ctr of Long Island
College Hospital Dept. of Social Work
339 Hicks St. Brooklyn, NY 11201
(718) 780-1899

The Roberts Wahls Bereavement Center
30 Broadway, Ste 210
Kingston, NY 12401
http://www.hospiceinc.org

The Sanctuary
2 Washington Square-Lobby Ste
SLarchmont, NY 10538
http://www.thesanctuaryforgrief.org

The Schnurmacher Family Bereavement
480 Old Westbury Rd
Roslyn Heights, NY 11577
http://www.northshorechildguidance.org

The Tree House Program
69 Main St
Tuckahoe, NY 10707
http://www.treehouse-bcw.org

Wave Riders Program for
Grieving Children & Teens of New York
(518) 694-4966

Wounded Healers
Bereavement Support Group
PO Box 1123
Auburn, NY 13021
http://www.woundedhealers.com

NORTH CAROLINA

Burke Hospice & Pallaitive Care
1721 Enon Road
Valdese, NC 28690
(828) 979-1601

Carousel Center
1100-c S Stratford Rd, Ste 201

Winston-Salem, NC 27103
http://www.carouselkids.org
Continuum Home Care & Hospice
3391 Henderason Dr. Ext.
Jacksonville, NC 28546
(910) 989-2682

Duke Community Bereavement
Services1001 Corporate Drive
Hillscorough, NC 27278
(919) 644-6869

Heart Songs of Four Seasons
Hospice & Palliative Care
P.O. Box 2395
Henersonville, NC 287-93
(828) 692-6178

Hospice of Rutherford Grief Center
P.O. Box 336
Forest City, NC 28043
(828) 245-0095

Kids Path of Hospice
& Palliative Care Center of Alam
914 Chapel Hill Road
Burlington, NC 27215
(336) 532-0123

Kids Path
2504 Summit Ave
Greensboro, NC 27405
http://www.hospice.org

KinderMourn, Inc.
1320 Harding Pl
Charlotte, NC 28204
http://www.kindermourn.org

Mountian Area Hospice - Kid's Path
68 Sweeten Creek Road
Asheville, NC 28803
(828) 251-0126

The Hospice
& Palliative Care Center of Mitchell
P.O. Box 38
Spruce Pine, NC 28777
(828) 765-5677

Reflections
A Caring Program for Children
1300 Saint Mary's St 4th Fl
Raleigh, NC 27605
http://www.hospiceofwake.org

The Sunrise Kids
725a Wellington Ave
Wilmington, NC 28401
http://www.hospiceandlifecarecenter.org

NORTH DAKOTA

Hospice
1380 S Columbia Rd
Grand Forks, ND 58206
http://www.altru.org

Hospice of the Red River Valley
1701 38th St SW Ste 201
Fargo, ND 58103
http://www.hrrv.org

OHIO

Akron Children's Hospital
One Perkins Square
Akron, OH 44308
(330) 543-8457

Aultman Grief Services for Children
2821 Woodlawn N.W.
Canton, OH 44708
(330) 479-4835

Bobby's Books
A Program of Ohio Hospice & Pall Care
555 Metro Place North, Ste. 650
Dublin, OH 43017
(614) 763-0036

Busch Family Funeral Chapels
Bereavement Care
4334 Pearl Rd
Cleveland, OH 44109
http://www.buschfuneral.com

Community-Mercy Hospice Bereavement Kid's Program
1343 N. Foundation Boulevard
Springfield, OH 455040
(937) 390-9665

Cornerstone of Hope
6600 Daisy Ave
Independence, OH 44131
http://www.cornerstoneofhope.org

Family Ties
682 E Buchtel Ave

Akron, OH 44304
http://www.childgc.org

Fernside: A Center for Grieving Children
4380 Malsbary Rd Ste 300
Cincinnati, OH 45242
http://www.fernside.org

Good Grief Club
1200 Sycamore Ln
Sandusky, OH 44870
http://www.steinhospice.org

Hope Center at Grady
561 W Central Ave
Delaware, OH 43015
http://www.gradyhospital.com

Hospice at Riverside and Grant
3595 Olentangy River Rd
Columbus,OH 43214
http://www.ohiohealth.com

Hospice of Cincinnati
4310 Cooper Rd
Cincinnati, OH 45242
http://www.hospiceofcincinnati.org

Hospice of Central Ohio
2269 Cherry Valley Road
Newark, OH 43055
(740) 344-0311

Hospice of Dayton
Pathways of Hope
324 Wilmington Ave
Dayton, OH 45420
http://www.hospicedayton.org

Hospice of North Central Ohio
1605 Ashland County Road 1095
Ashland, OH 44805
http://www.hospiceofnorthcentralohio.org

Hospice & Palliative
Care of Greateer Wayne County
Wooster, OH 44691
(330) 263-4899

Hospice of the Western Reserve
29101 Health Campus Dr Ste 400
Westlake, OH 44145
http://www.hospicewr.org

Hospice of the Western Reserve
300 E 185th St

Cleveland, OH 44119
http://www.hospicewr.org
Hospice of the Western Reserve
5786 Heisley Rd
Mentor, OH 44060
http://www.hospicewr.org

Hospice of the Western Reserve
4110 Warrensville Center Rd
Blding A Lobby A
Warrensville Heights, OH 44122
http://www.hopsicewr.org

Hospice of the Western Reserve
10645 Euclid Ave
Cleveland, OH 44106
http://www.hospicewr.org

Hospice of the Valley
Bereavement Resource Center
3736 Boardman - Canfield Road
Canfield, OH 44406
(330) 788-1992

Joel's Place for Children
195 Aspenwood Dr
Moreland Hills, OH 44022
http://www.joelsplaceforchildren.com

Mending Hearts
225 Ludlow Street
Hammilton, OH 45011
(513) 896-4357

Mount Carmel Hospice Evergreen Center
1144 Dublin Rd
Columbus, OH 43215
http://www.hchs.org

Oak Tree Corner, Inc.
2312 Far Hills Ave Box 108
Dayton, OH 45419
http://www.oaktreecorner.com

Routsong Funeral Home Stepping Stones
2100 E. Stroop Road
Kittering, OH 45429
(937) 293-4137

Project Hope
1510 N Main St
Dayton, OH 45406
937-277-7828

Stein Hospice
1200 Sycamore Line

Sandusky, OH 44870
http://www.steinhospice.org
St. Rita's Hospice Trails
770 W. North Street
Lima, OH 45801
(419) 226-9064

The Elizabeth Severance Prentiss
Berevment Center
Hospice of the Western Reserve
19201 Villaview Road
Cleveland, OH 44119
(216) 486-6838

The Gathering Place
23300 Commerce Pk
Beachwood, OH 44122
(216) 595-9546

The Treehouse
2421 Auburn Ave
Cincinnati, OH 45219
(513) 731-3346

Valley Hospice Inc.
380 Summit Ave
Steubenville, OH 43952
(740) 283-7487

Willow Wood
41 E Main
Amelia, OH 45147
http://www.willowwood.org

Your Heart to Mine
561 W Central Ave
Delaware, OH 43015
614-368-5223

OKLAHOMA

A Place of Hope
307 S Seneca
Bartlesville, OK 74006
http://www.geocities.com/aplaceofhope

Calm Waters Center
3525 NW 56th St Ste a-150
Oklahoma City, OK 73112
http://www.calmwaters.org

The Kid's Place
PO Box 258
Edmond, OK 73083
http://www.kidsplace.org

The Kids Place of Edmond
801 S Bryant
Edmond, OK 73034
405-844-5437

OREGON

Caring Hearts Support Group
721 SE Third
Pendleton, OR 97801
http://www.thecaringhearts.org

**Compassionate Friends
Portland Chapter**
PO Box 3065
Portland, OR 97208
http://www.portlandtcf.org

**Courageous Kids/
Hospice of Sacred Heart**
1121 Fairfield Ave
Eugene, OR 97402
http://www.peacehealth.org

The Dougy Center
P.O. Box 86852
Portland, OR 97286
(503) 775-5683

Early Childhood Council
2001 SW Nye Ave
Pendleton, OR 97801
541-966-3133

Good Grief- Lovejoy Hospice
939 SE 8th St
Grants Pass, OR 97526
http://www.lovejoyhospice.org

Hope House
3107 Grand Ave
Astoria, OR 97103
503-325-6754

Hospice of Bend/La Pine
2075 NE Wyatt Ct
Bend, OR 97701
http://www.hospicebendlapine.org

Light House Center
1620 Thompson Rd
Coos Bay, OR 97420
541-269-2986

Me, Too. & Company
PO Box 10796
Portland, OR 97296
http://www.oregonhospice.org

**Mother Oak's Child
Center for Grieving Children**
1015 3rd St NW
Salem, OR 97304
http://www.wvh.org

Mourning Resources, Inc.
PO Box 82573
Portland, OR 97202
503-777-0433

My Friend's House, Inc.
1293 Wall St #1339
Bend, OR 97701
541-385-0609 (fax)

St. Anthony Hospital Hospice
1601 SE CT Ave
Pendleton, OR 97801
541-278-6571

Winterspring
PO Box 8169
Medford, OR 97501
http://www.winterspring.org

PENNSYLVANIA

Caring Place
620 Stanwix St
Pittsburgh, PA 15222
http://www.wpacaringfoundation.com

**Allegheny General Hospital Center
for Traumatic Grief Treatments**
4 Allecheny Center, 8th Floor
Pittsburgh, PA 15212
(412) 330-4328

Camp Connections
154 Hindman Road
Butler, PA 16001
(724) 431-3520

Cancer Caring Center
4117 Liberty Avenue
Pittsburgh, PA 15224
(412) 622-1212

**Center for Grieving
Children, Teens & Families**
Erie Ave at Front St
Philadelphia, PA 19134
http://www.grievingchildren.org

Center for Loss and Bereavement
3874 Skippack Pike
Skippack, PA 19474
http://www.bereavementcenter.org

Children's Hospital of Philadelphia
34th & Civic Center Blvd
Philadelphia, PA 19104
http://www.chop.edu

Coping Kids Program
685 Good Dr
Lancaster, PA 17604
http://www.hospiceoflancaster.org

Highmark Caring Place
620 Stanwix Street
Pittsburgh, PA 15222
(814) 871-6853

Hospice Care, Inc.
343 E Roy Furman Hwy #107
Waynesburg, PA 15370
http://www.welnet.org

Jewish Family Service
3333 N. Front Street
Harrisburg, PA 17110
(717) 233-1681

Mommy's Light Lives On
PO Box 494
Lionville, PA 19353
http://www.mommyslight.org

Olivia's House
830 S George St
York, PA 17403
http://www.oliviashouse.org

Peter's Place
PO Box 177
Berwyn, PA 19312
http://www.petersplaceonline.org

Pinnacle Health Hospice
3705 Elmwood Dr
Harrisburg, PA 17110

http://www.pinnaclehealth.org

Precious Gems Counseling Services
231 S Easton Rd Third Fl
Glenside, PA 19038
http://www.preciousgems.org

Safe Harbor Program
2510 Maryland Rd
Willow Grove, PA 19090
http://www.amh.org/healthsrv/wcsafhar

St. Luke's VNA Hospice
1510 Valley Center Pkwy Ste 200
Bethlehem, PA 18017
www.vnaofstlukes.org

Sun Home Health Hospice
PO Box 232
Northumberland, PA 17857
http://www.sunhomehealth.com

Rhode Island Friends Way
765 West Shore Rd
Warwick, RI 02889
http://www.friendsway.org

**The Center for Grieving Children,
Teens & Families**
Erie Avenue at Front St.
Philadelphia, PA 19134
(215) 427-6767

The Center for Loss and Bereavement
3847 Skippack Pike
Skippack, PA 19474
(610) 222-4110

**TIDES - Support Program
for Grieving Children**
P.O. Box 1251
State College, PA 16804
(814) 231-7112

Vitas Innovative Hospice Care
1740 Walton Road #100
Blue Bell, PA 19422
(610) 260-6020

RHODE ISLAND

Friends Way
765 West Shore Rd
Warwick, RI 02889
http://www.friendsway.org

SOUTH CAROLINA

Good Grieving:
Helping Children and Teens
7 Richland Medical Park Dr
Columbia, SC 29203
http://www.sccancercenter.org

Friends of Caroline Hospice
Child Bereavement Program
1110-13 St.
Port Royal, SC 29935
(843) 525-6257

Hospice & Community Care
PO Box 993
Rock Hill, SC 29731
http://www.hospicecommunitycare.org

OMH Hospice of the Euothills
390 Keowee School Road
Seneca, SC 29678
(864) 882-8940

Palmetto Richland SC Cancer Center
7 Richland Medical Park
Columbia, SC 29203
(803) 434-4566

TENNESSEE

Babtist Trinity Center for Good Grief
1059 Cresthaven Road
Memphis, TN 38119
(901) 767-6767

KICS Inc. (Kids in Crisis Support)
2455 Sutherland Avenue
Knoxville, TN 37922
(865) 541-5038

The Grief Center fo Alive Hospice
1718 Patterson St.
Nashville, TN 37203
(615) 963-4732

TEXAS

Bo's Place
5501 Austin St
Houston, TX 77004
http://www.bosplace.org

Building Bridges
PO Box 471
San Angelo, TX 76902
325-658-6524

Building Bridges
P..O. box 4804
Wichita Falls, TX 76308
(940) 691-0982

Camp El Tesoro de la Vida
2700 Meacham Blvd
Forth Worth, TX 76137
http://www.firsttexascampfire.org

Children's Grief Center of El Paso
123 W Mills, Ste 650
El Paso, TX 79901
http://www.cgcelpaso.org

Children's Bereavement Center
of South Texas
332 W. Craig
San Antonio, TX 78212
(210) 736-4847

Dallas Kids GriefWorks
6320 LBJ Freeway Ste 121
Dallas, TX 75240
http://www.christianservices-sw.org

Griefworks through Christian
Works for Children
6320 LBJ Freeway #122
Dallas, TX 75240
(972) 960-9981

Hope Hospice Children's Grief Program
611 N. Walnut Avenue
New Braunfels, TX 78130
(830) 625-7525

Hospice Austin
4107 Spicewood Springs Rd, Ste 100
Austin, TX 78759
http://www.hospiceaustin.org

Journey of Hope Grief Support Center, Inc.
3900 W 15th Ste 306
Piano, TX 75075
http://www.johgriefsupport.org

Project Joy and Hope for Texas
PO Box 5111

Pasadena, TX 77508
http://www.joyandhope.org

**The Children's Bereavement Center
of South Texas**
332 W Craig
San Antonio, TX 78212
http://www.cbcst.org

The Warm Place
809 Lipscomb St
Forth Worth, TX 76104
http://www.thewarmplace.org

Wings Childrens Grief Program
4111 University Blvd
Tyler, TX 75701
http://www.hospice-etex.com

Wings Program
8811 Gaylord Ste 100
Houston, TX 77024
http://www.houstonhospice.org

UTAH

Canary Garden
PO Box 53
Lehi, UT 84043
http://www.canarygarden.org

**Caring Connections: A Hope
& Comfort in Grief Program**
Salt Lake City, UT 84112
(801) 585-9522

Primary Children's Medical Center
100 Medical Dr
Salt Lake City, UT 84113
801-588-3483

The Family Summit Foundation
560 39th St
South Ogden, UT 84403
http://www.familysummit.com

The Grief Center
1050 E South Temple
Salt Lake City, UT 84102
801-350-4191

The Sharing Place
1695 E 3300 South
Salt Lake City, UT 84106
http://www.thesharingplace.com

VIRGINIA

Fairfax County Mental Health
8348 Traford Ln Ste 400
Springfield, VA 22152
703-866-2119

Good Samaritan Hospice
3825 Electric Rd Ste A
Roanoke, VA 24018
http://www.goodsamaritanhospice.org

Grief Resource Center
3932 Springfield Road
Glen Allen, VA 23060
(804) 360-2884

Jewish Family Service of Tidewater, Inc.
260 Grayson Rd
Virginia Beach, VA 23462
http://www.jfshamptonroads.org

**Kids' Haven:
A Center for Grieving Children**
2102 Rivermont Ave
Lynchburg, VA 24503
434-845-4072

Kidz n Grief
2 Bernardine Dr
Newport News, VA 23602
757-886-6613

The Comfort Zone Camp
2101 A Westmoreland St
Richmond, VA 23230
(804) 377-3430
http://www.ComfortZoneCamp.org

WASHINGTON

Annie Tran Centers for Grief & Loss
2001 Paterson Rd
Prosser, WA 99350
509-786-7100

Bridges: A Center for Grieving Children
310 N K St
Tacoma, WA 98403
http://www.mbch.org

Camp Amanda
PO Box 2026
Walla Walla, WA 99362
http://www.wwhospice.org

Cedar Center
1200 W Fairview Ave
Colfax, WA 99111
http://www.whitmanhospice.org

Center for Counseling and Development
1021 Legion Wy SE
Olympia, WA 98501
http://www.chhh.org

Children Grieve Too
451 SW 10th St #215
Renton, WA 98055
http://www.scn.org

Community Home Health and Hospice
1035 11th Ave
Longview,WA 98632
http://www.chhh.org

Cork's Place
2108 W. Entiat Avenue
Kennewick, WA 99336
(509) 783-7416

Good Samaratin Hospice
PO Box 1247
Puyallup, WA 98371
253-841-5668

Griefbusters
PO Box 2026
Walla Walla, WA 99362
http://www.wwhospice.org

GriefWorks: A Bereavement Resource
PO Box 912
Auburn, WA 98071
http://www.griefworks.org

Journey Program
4800 Sandpoint Wy NE
Seattle, WA 98105
http://www.seattlechildrens.org

Kids Grief Group
3100 Bucklin Hill Rd #201
Silverdale, WA 98383
http://www.hospiceofkitsapcounty.org

Lisa's Kids
1225 E Sunset Dr Ste 145
Bellingham, WA 98226
360-715-2597

Providence Hospice of Seattle
425 Pontius Ave N Ste 200
Seattle, WA 98109
http://www.providence.org

**Providence Hospice
of Snohomish County**
2731 Wetmore Ave Ste 520
Everett, WA 98201
http://www.providence.org

Rise n' Shine
417 23rd Ave S
Seattle, WA 98144
http://www.risenshine.org

Sound Care Kids
PO Box 5008
Olympia, WA 98509
http://www.providence.org

Stepping Stones
PO Box 1600
Vancouver, WA 98663
360-696-5120

The Chaplaincy
2108 W Entiat
Kennewick, WA 99336
http://www.tricitieschaplaincy.org

The Good Grief Center
1610 5th St
Wenatchee, WA 98801
http://www.goodgriefcenter.org

The Journey Program
P.O. Box 5371
Seattle, WA 98105
(206) 987-2062

WICS WINGS
PO Box 66896
Seattle, WA 98166
http://www.widowedinformation.org

**Widowed Information
and Consultation Services**
P.O. Box 66896
Seattle, WA 98166
(206) 241-5650

WISCONSIN

Beloit Regional Hospice
655 Third Street, Suite 200
Beloit, WI 53511
(608) 363-7421

Camp Hope
301 Florence Dr
Stevens Point, WI 54481
http://www.camphopeforkids.org

Care Connection-
Community Memorial Hospital
W180 N8085 Town Hall Rd
Menomonee Falls, WI 53052
http://www.communitymemorial.com

Children's Hospital of Wisconsin
9000 W Wisconsin Ave
Milwaukee, WI 53201
http://www.chw.org

Kyles' Korner
4800 S 84th St
Milwaukee, WI 53228
http://www.kyleskorner.com

Margaret Ann's Place
2522 63rd St
Kenosha, WI 53142
http://www.margaretannsplace.org

My Good Mourning Place
4005 W Oklahoma Ave
Milwaukee, WI 53215
414-643-5678

St. Luke's Hospital
2900 W Oklahoma Ave
Milwaukee, WI 53215
414-649-6634

Unity Hospice and Palliative Care
916 Willard Dr Ste 100
Green Bay, WI 54304
http://www.unityhospice.org

AUSTRALIA

A Friends Place
PO Box 584
Terrigal, NSW 2260, Australia

Nelson Bros. Funeral Services
Footscray 3011 Victoria, Australia

CANADA

Canuck Place
1690 Matthews Ave
Vancouver, BC V6J2T2, Canada
http://www.canuckplace.org

Cardinal Funeral Homes
715 Dovercourt Rd
Toronto, ON M6H 2W7, Canada
http://www.cardinalfuneralhomes.com

Good Grief Workshop
for Children and Adolescents
1297 chemin de la foret
Montreal, QC H2V 2P9, Canada
http://www.mountroyalacem.com

Grief Resource Network of Nova
Scotia5530 Auxillery Place Unit 408
Halifax, NS B3J 1J3, Canada

Griefworks BC
4500 Oak St Rm E405
Vancouver, BC V6H 3N1, Canada
http://www.griefworksbc.com

Grieving Children at Seasons Centre
4 Alliance Blvd Unit #7
Barrie, ON L4M 5J1, Canada
http://www.grievingchildren.com

Kids Griefworks,
Canadian Mental Health Association
1400 Windsor Ave
Windsor, Ontario, ON N8X3L9. Canada

Langley Hospice
20088-40 A Ave
Langley , BC V3A 2Y6, Canada
http://www.mypage.direct.ca/l/hospice/

McGill University Health Centre
2300 Tupper St
Montreal, QC PQ H3H 1P3, Canada

Mission Hospice Society
7324 Hurd St
Mission, BC 2V 3H5, Canada

Pilgrims Hospice Society
9808 148th St
Edmonton, AB T59 3E8, Canada
http://www.pilgramshospice.ca

Surrey Hospice Society
13857 68th Ave
Surrey, BC V3W 2G9, Canada
http://www.surveyhospice.com

The Carly Centre for Grieving Children
728 Anderson St
Whitby, ON LIN 0A4, Canada

The Edith Fox Life & Loss Centre
Picton, K0K 2T0, Canada
http://www.edithfoxcentre.org

The Lighthouse Program
435 Lakeshore Rd E
Oakville, ON L6J 1K1, Canada

Victorian Order of Nurses
422 Beaconsfield Blvd
Beaconsfield, H9W4B7, Canada

White Rock Hospice
15510 Russell Ave
White Rock, BC V4B 2R3
http://www.whiterockhospice.org

England

**Barney's Support
for Bereaved Young People**
1B King St
Kempston, Bedfordshire, NK42 8BW,
England

Winston's Wish
Bayhill Rd
Cheltenham, GL50 3AW, England
http://www.winstonswish.org.uk

Germany

Bjorn Schulz Stiftung
Wilhlem-Wolff-Str 36-38
13156 Berlin, Germany
http://www.bjoern-Schulz-Stiftung.de

Domino-Zentrum fur trauernde Kinder e.V
Auf dem Broich 24
51519 Odenthal,Koln, Germany
http://www.zentrakin.de

**Evangelische Jugend
Munchen-Region Nord**
Birkerstr 19
Munchen, 80939, Germany

**Zentrum fur Trauernde Kinder
e.V** Elisabethstrasse 135
Bremen, 28217, Germany

Ireland

Rainbows Ireland
Crumlin Rd
Dublin, 12 Ireland
http://www.rainbowsireland.com

Japan

Ashinaga Ilkueiki/Rainbow House
1-7-3 Honjo-cho
Higiashi-Nada-Ku, Kobe, Japan
http://www.ashinaga.org

Asobo
8-14 Sumiyoshi-cho
Tokyo, 162-0065, Japan

Shanti Nilaya Okinawa
1-19-5 Higawa Naha
Okinawa, 900-0022, Japan

New Zealand

Skylight
PO Box 7309
Wellington South, New Zealand
http://www.skylight.org.nz

Switzerland

As' Trame
Ave Jomini 5
Lausanne, 1004 Switzerland
http://www.astrame.ch

United Kingdom

St. Christopher's Hospice
51-5g Lawrie Park Rd
London, SE26 6DZ, United Kingdom

THE FOLLOWING ARE GRIEF CAMPS ACROSS THE GLOBE

ALABAMA

Wiregrass Hospice
2740 Headland Avenue
Dothan, Alabama 36303
(334) 792-1100
http://www.wiregrasshospice.org/brave

Camp Newsong: For Grieving Children
Alabama Foundation for Oncology
P.O. Box 660833
Birmingham, AL 35266-0833
(205) 877-2225
http://www.alfoundationforoncology.
org/campnewsong.php

Camp Comfort
http://www.campcomfortsite.com

ARIZONA

Hospice Caring, Inc.
http://hospicecaring.org

Camp Solari
Phoenix, AZ
http://www.solarihospice.com

Camp Erin - Phoenix, AZ
Stepping Stones of Hope
(602) 264-7520
lisaw@steppingstonesofhope.org

CALIFORNIA

Camp HUG–Sierra Hospice
P.O. Box 95
Chester, CA 96020
(530) 258-3412
www.sierrahospice.org

Camp Erin - Palm Springs, CA
The Mourning Star Center of the VNAIC
(760) 836-0360
Pamela Gabbay

COLORADO

Camp Cascade
Pagosa Springs, CO
(970) 382-2011
http://pagosarally.com

Camp Comfort
Evergreen, CO
http://www.mtevans.org

DC

Camp Forget-Me-Not
Washington, DC
http://www.wendtcenter.org

TAPS-Tragedy Assistance Program
910 17th St NW Ste 800
Washington, DC 20006
(800)959-8277

MONTANA

Camp Francis Peace Hospice of Montana
1101 26th St South
Great Falls, MT 59404
(406)455-3054

Terrapin Center Grief Resources
The Center for Integrative Care
336 W Spruce St
Missoula, MT 59802
(406)721-2860

IDAHO

Camp Erin - Boise, ID
Life's Doors Hospice
(208) 275-0000
zimerman@lifesdoors.com

INDIANA

Camp Kesem
Notre Dame, IN
http://www.campkesem-nd.org

IOWA

Amanda the Panda
1000 73rd St. Suite 12
Des Moines, Iowa 50311
http://www.amandathepanda.org

MASSACHUSETTS

Handi Kids
Bridgewater, MA
http://www.handikids.org

NEVADA

Camp Solace
Lake Tahoe, NV
P.O. Box 2944, Reno, Nevada 89505
(775) 324-7723
www.solacetree.org

NEW YORK

Camp Good Days & Spcial Times
Branchport, NY
(585) 624-5555
www.campgooddays.org

East End Hospice - Camp Good Grief
Westhampton Beach, NY
http://www.eeh.org

OHIO

**Fernside: A Center for Grieving Children
Camp WeBelong**
4380 Malsbary Rd Ste 300
Cincinnati, OH 45242
(513) 745-0111
http://www.fernside.org

OREGON

Camp Erin - Portland, OR
Providence Hospice of Oregon
(503) 215-4691
Marilyn.Schulte@providence.org

PHILADELPHIA

**University of Pennsylvania Wissahick-
on Hospice**
(610) 617-2499 ext. 7519
Andrea.McLean@uphs.upenn.edu

TENNESSEE

Baptist Memorial Health Care Corporation
350 North Humphreys Blvd.
Memphis, TN 38120
http://www.baptistonline.org

TEXAS

**Camp Agape Bereavement
Camp for Children**
Lampasas, Texas
http://www.campagapetexas.org
(512) 756-7353"

VIRGINIA

Comfort Zone Camp
2101-A Westmoreland St.
Richmond, VA 23230
(866) 488-5679
www.comfortzonecamp.org

WASHINGTON

Camp Erin - The Moyer Foundation
Woodinville, Washington
http://www.moyerfoundation.org

**BRIDGES:
A Center for Grieving Children**
P.O. Box 5299
Tacoma, WA 98415-0299
253-272-8266
heather.neal@multicare.org

Camp Erin - Snohomish County, WA
Stanwood, WA 98292
Providence Hospice of Snohomish County
425-261-4738
Debi.Schmidt@providence.org

OTHER

Camp Good Grief
http://www.baptistonline.org

Camp Little Light of Mine
http://www.hospiceofthevalley.com

Camp Nabe
http://www.hospiceofhuntington.org

Camp ReLEAF
http://dhch.dukehealth.org

IRELAND

The Barretstown Camp Fund Ltd.
Ireland
http://www.barretstown.org

Memory Collage

Goals:
To create a collage of memories or feelings about the person who died.

Age Group(s): All ages

The Activity:

- Display a variety of magazines or catalogs (make sure you check the content).

- Provide different color poster boards, crayons, glue, paper, markers, tape, scissors, etc.

- Have participants cut out pictures, items, people, animals, words, etc., that remind them of their loved one.

- Have participants paste them on a poster board.

Ask the group if they want to share. This is a great project for memorabilia for the group to bring next time to group or showcase in a grieving center, classroom, or home. Group members can write poems, put pictures up of the deceased, draw pictures, write a letter or they can take it home and either work on it or bring it back to group.

Commemoration Game

Goals:
To have children share their loss with others in group and have fun too.

Age Group(s): All ages

The Activity:

- You will need a bag of M&M's, Skittles or any other colored candies that the children are not allergic to.

- List of questions for each color such as:

- Red – share a happy memory, Blue – Give an example of something that has changed since your _____ died.
    - Each color is a different question.
    - They can make up the questions or you can provide the questions.
    - They can participate only if they want to.
    - The facilitator will model the start of the game.
    - After the circle is completed everyone can eat their candy.
    - There are many variations – Be creative!

Creating Ways to Grieve

Goals:

To have teenagers recognize and talk about things to do instead of hurting while they are grieving.

Age Group: 10 to 18

The Activity:

Discuss in group with children and teens what they can do to not hurt themselves or others while they are grieving. Use the list below and write them on note cards or put them on a board or wall:

- Rip up old phone books
- Punch pillows
- Throw a tennis ball or other balls that are safe against a wall
- Dance
- Kick pillows or stuffed animals
- Run
- Find bubble wrap, then stomp on it
- Write letters to the deceased
- Take a karate class
- Kick a soccer ball into a net or a wall
- Go for a bike ride
- Paint
- Find styrofoam and break it, kick it, and punch it
- Skip rocks in a river, lake, stream, or pond

Obituaries

Goals:

To allow group members to write in their own words an obituary for whoever died.

Age Group: 8 to 18

The Activity:

- Bring in an example of an obituary from numerous newspapers, or have the children or teens bring one in from the past.
- Bring in paper, journals and pens.
- Talk about obituaries.
- Ask questions about their own family's obituary if they brought one in.
- Ask children if they could write an obituary of their own, what would it say.
- Ask children and teens if they would like to share their obituary.

SUGGESTED READINGS FOR CHILDREN AND TEENS

AGES 3 TO 7

Brown, L. (1998). *When Dinosaurs Die: A Guide to Understanding Death.* Boston: Little Brown & Co. (explaining to young children the simple language of death).

De Paola, T. (1973). *Nana Upstairs and Nana Downstairs.* New York: Putman. (grandparent death).

Goldman, L. (1998). *Bart Speaks Out: Breaking the Silence on Suicide.* Western Psychological Services: Los Angeles.

Harris, R. (2001). *Goodbye Mousie.* New York: McElderry Books (pet loss).

Johnson, J. (2005). *Tell Me, Papa: Answers to Questions Children ask about Death and Dying.* Omaha, NE. The Centering Corporation.

Rogers, F. (1998). *When a Pet Dies.* New York: Putnam & Grosset Group. (death of a pet).

Varley, S. (1984). *Badger's Parting Gifts.* New York: Lothrop, Lee & Shepard Books. (death of a friend).

Vorst, J. (1971). *The Tenth Good Thing about Barney.* Anthenaeum. (a book on commemorating).

AGES 8 TO 12

Alexander, A. (2002). *A Mural for Mamita.* Omaha, NE. The Centering Corporation. (grandmother death).

Carney, K. (1995). *Barklay and Eve; What is Cancer, Anyway?* Wethersfield: Karen Carney (a book explaining cancer to young children).

The Dougy Center. (1997). *Helping Children Cope with Death.* Portland, OR.

Goldman, L. (2006). *Children Also Grieve: Talking About Death and Healing.* London: Jessica Kingsley Publishers.

Goble, P. (1989). *Beyond The Ridge.* New York: Bradley Press. (funeral issues).

Johnson, J. (2004). *Keys to Helping Children Deal with Grief.* Omaha, NE: The Centering Corporation. (Helping children grieve).

Parga, E. (2007). *Love Never Stops.* Reno, NV. The Solace Tree. (A memory book for grieving children).

Mellonie, B. (1983). *Lifetimes: The Beautiful Way to Explain Death to Children.* New York: Bantam Books. (explaining death through the process of life – plants, animals, people).

Smith, H. (2004). *When a Child you know is Grieving.* Kansas City: Beacon Hill Press (when children are grieving – for parents).

Smith, H. (2006). *What Does That Mean? A Dictionary for Grieving Children.* Nebraska: The Centering Corporation.

AGES 13 TO 18

Devita-Raeburn, E. (2004). *The Empty Room: Surviving the Loss of a Brother or Sister at any age.* NY: Scribner. (death of a sibling).

The Dougy Center. (1999). *Helping Teens Cope with Death.* Portland, OR.

Dower, L. (2001). *I Will Remember You.* New York, NY: Scholastic Inc. (death of a teen friend).

Gootman, Marilyn. (1994). *When a Friend Dies: A Book for Teens about Grieving and Healing.* Minneapolis: Free Spirit Publishing.

Grollman, E. (1993). *Straight Talk about Death for Teenagers: How to Cope with Losing Someone you Love.* Boston: Beacon Press. (a book about suicide).

Hughes, L. (2006). *You Are Not Alone: Teens Talk about Life after the Loss of a Parent.* Scholastic. (stories from grief camp).

Scrivani, M. (1991). *When Death Walks In.* Omaha, NE: The Centering Corporation (teen grief).

Traisman, E. (1992). *Fire in My Heart: Ice in My Veins.* Omaha: Centering Corporation (a journal for teens).

BOOKS FOR ADULTS

Grollman, E. (1991). *Talking About Death: A Dialogue between Parent and Child.* Boston: Beacon Press. (starting the conversation about death for teenagers).

Gilbert, R. (1999). *Finding your Way after your Parent Dies: Hope for Grieving Adults.* Notre Dame, IN: Ave Maria Press.

Harris, M. (1996). *The Loss that is Forever: The Lifelong Impact of the Early Death of a Mother or Father.* New York: Plume.

Lavin, J. (2001). *Special Kids need Special Parents: A Resource for Parents of Children with Special Needs.* New York: Berkley Books.

Ross, C. (2005). *Pet Loss and Children: Establishing a Healthy Foundation.* New York: Routledge (pet loss).

Schlessel, W. (1997). *When a Parent has Cancer: A Guide to Caring for your Children.* Compassion Books. (helping children through the upheaval battle of having a parent who has been diagnosed with cancer).

Schuurman, D. (2003). **Never the Same: Coming to Terms with the Death of a Parent**. NY: St Martins Press. (death of a parent for adults.

Wezeman, P. (2001). *Finding Your way after Your Child Dies.* Notre Dame, IN. Ave Maria Press (death of a child).

BOOKS FOR TEACHERS AND COUNSELORS

Cassini, K., Rogers, J. (1989). *Death in the Classroom.* Cincinnati: Grief Work.

The Dougy Center. (1998). *Helping the Grieving Student: A Guide for Teachers.* Portland, OR.

Fitzgerald, H. (1993). *The Grieving Child.* New York: Simon & Schuster. (helping the grieving child).

Goldman, L. (2001). *Life and Loss: A Guide to Help Grieving Children.* 2nd Ed. New York: Taylor and Francis Publishers.

Goldman, L. (2005). *Raising our Children to be Resilient: A Guide to Helping Children Cope with Trauma in Today's World.* NY: Brunner-Routledge. (grief in the classroom and at home).

Grollman, E. (1998). *Suicide: Prevention, Intervention, Postvention.* Boston: Beacon Press. (death of a suicide).

Jarratt, C.S. (1982). *Helping Children Cope with Separation & Loss.* Boston: Harvard Common Press. (talking to children about loss).

Wray, T.J. (2003). *Living Through Grief when an Adult Brother or Sister Dies: Surviving the Death of a Sibling.* New York: Three Rivers Press.

BOOKS FOR CHILDREN AND TEENS DEALING WITH CANCER

Heegaard, M. (1991). *When Someone has a Very Serious Illness.* Minneapolis, MN: Fairview Press. (a workbook for children of all school aged children dealing with loved ones with cancer).

Heegaard, M. (2003). *Beyond the Rainbow: A Workbook for Children in the Advanced Stages of a Very Serious Illness.* MN: Fairview Press.

Jonah, A. (1999). *Transitions Along the Way: A Guide to the Dying Process for Children and Young Adults.*

Hershey, M. (1999). *Oncology, Stupology: I Want to go Home!* Butterfly Press.

Nussbaum, K. (1998). *Preparing the Children: Information and Ideas for Families Facing Terminally Illness and Death.*

The Dougy Center (1997). *What about the Kids? Understanding their Needs in the Funeral Planning & Services.* Portland OR.

Powers, L. (1994). *Helping Children Heal from Loss: A Keepsake Book of Special Memories.*

Wolfelt, A. (2003). *How I Feel: A Coloring Book for Grieving Children.*

ABOUT THE AUTHOR

Author of *Love Never Stops*, two-time cancer survivor and pediatric thanatologist Emilio Parga, M.A. is the founder and executive director of The Solace Tree – Child and Adolescent Center for Grief and Loss in Reno, NV. Emilio Parga serves as a bereavement consultant to Washoe County Department of Social Services, Washoe County School District, local hospitals, churches and funeral homes. He provides in-service credits, trainings and lectures on peer support groups related to children and teens grieving a loss through death.

He is a member of the Association for Death Education and Counseling (ADEC), the National Alliance for Grieving Children, American Academy of Pediatrics and the American Professional Society on the Abuse of Children (APSAC). Emilio lives in Reno, NV with his wife and son.

THE

Solace Tree

Child and Adolescent Center
for Grief and Loss

www.solacetree.org